CAMBRIDGE INTRODUCTION TO THE HISTORY OF MANKIND

Europe Round the World

Trevor Cairns

CAMBRIDGE UNIVERSITY PRESS
Cambridge
London   New York   New Rochelle
Melbourne   Sydney

Published by the Press Syndicate of the University of Cambridge
The Pitt Building, Trumpington Street, Cambridge CB2 1RP
32 East 57th Street, New York, NY 10022, USA
296 Beaconsfield Parade, Middle Park, Melbourne 3206, Australia

© Cambridge University Press 1981

First published 1981

Set, printed and bound in Great Britain by
Fakenham Press Limited, Fakenham, Norfolk

British Library cataloguing in publication data
Cairns, Trevor
Europe round the world. – (Cambridge introduction to the history of mankind; 9).
1. Europe – Colonies – History
I. Title II. Series
909.7   JV135   79–41598
ISBN 0 521 22710 0

Maps and diagrams by Reg Piggott

Illustrations in this volume are reproduced by kind permission of the following:
Front cover, The Trustees of the Wedgwood Museum, Barlaston, Staffs; p. 4 (left) National Gallery of Canada, Ottawa; p. 4 (right) Thomas Jefferson Memorial Foundation, Monticello; pp. 5, 54, 60 (left), 62 (bottom), 66 (bottom right) Library of Congress, Washington; pp. 7, 9 (bottom), 10 Copyright Bibliothèque royale Albert 1er, Bruxelles; p. 9 (top left) Ampliaciones y Reproducciones MAS; p. 9 (top right) Instituto Nacional Sanmartiniano, Buenos Aires; p. 13 Museo Nacional de Bellas Artes, Buenos Aires; p. 14 (top) Brooke Bond Oxo Ltd.; pp. 14 (bottom), 35, 43 (right), 66 (top), 82, 91 BBC Hulton Picture Library; pp. 15, 41 (bottom) The National Maritime Museum, London; pp. 18, 20 (centre right) Provincial Archives of British Columbia; p. 20 (bottom) British Columbia Government; p. 20 (top) Canadian Pacific Railway; p. 22 (bottom left) The Australian Information Service, London; p. 22 (bottom right) Australia Post; p. 22 (top) National Library of Australia; p. 30 Courtesy of the Africana Museum, Johannesburg; pp. 31, 33, 36 India Office Library; p. 37 (top) from Charles Allen, *Raj, A Scrapbook of British India*, Andre Deutsch Ltd., 1977; pp. 37 (below), 80 *The Illustrated London News*; pp. 40, 41 (top) Weidenfeld & Nicolson Ltd, London; pp. 42, 49 (top), 78 Roger-Viollet, Paris; p. 43 from *The First Chinese Embassy to the West*: The Journals of Kuo Sung-T'ao and Liu Hsi-Hung and Chnag-Te-yi, translated and annotated by J. D. Frodsham, Oxford University Press, 1974; p. 45 Japan Information Centre, London; pp. 46, 50 (below), back cover The Trustees of the British Museum, London; pp. 48, 50 (top) Crown copyright: Victoria and Albert Museum, London; p. 49 (bottom) International Society for Educational Information, Tokyo, Japan; p. 51 A. E. Matthews: *Pencil Sketches of Montana*, 1868, plate XI, Montana Historical Society, Helena; p. 52 (bottom) Hudson's Bay Co., Canada; p. 52 (top) Walters Art Gallery, Maryland; p. 53 Anne S. K. Brown Military Collection; p. 55 The Smithsonian Institution, Washington; p. 57 New York Historical Society; p. 60 (right) The Bettman Archive Inc., New York; p. 61 Idaho State Historical Society; p. 62 (top) Kansas State Historical Society; p. 63 Yale University Library; p. 64 U.S. National Archives and Records Service; p. 65 (top left) Carnegie Library of Pittsburgh; p. 65 (bottom) The Carnegie Dunferminile Trust; pp. 65 (top right), 72 (left) Trevor Cairns; p. 66 (bottom left) The Granger Collection, New York; pp. 67, 68 Museum of the City of New York; pp. 71, 76 (left) Novosti Press Agency, London; p. 75 from L. Blanch, *Sabres of Paradise*, John Murray, 1960; p. 76 (right) Tretyakov Gallery, Moscow; p. 77 John Massey-Stewart; p. 83 (top) William Fehr Collection, Cape Town; p. 86 *Jugend*, 1896; p. 87 Madame Tussaud's, London; pp. 88, 89, 90 National Army Museum; p. 93 (top) Fotomas Index; p. 93 (bottom) Courtauld Institute Galleries, London.

front cover: *When Europeans first spread overseas they accepted slavery and the slave trade as normal, but by the later eighteenth century many saw them as an evil that ought to be swept away. In 1787 Josiah Wedgwood, the famous potter, produced and distributed this china medallion, bearing the emblem of the anti-slavery movement.*

back cover: *To people of other civilisations the European intruders were strange-looking persons in quaint garments who identified themselves by flags with curious patterns. This is how the Japanese print-maker Sadahide saw a gathering of representatives of five Western nations (the U.S.A., Britain, France, Russia, the Netherlands) in Tokyo soon after Japan had been forced to open her ports to foreigners.*

Contents

1 Republics of the New World *p.4*
Fall or rise? *p.4*
The U.S.A. begins to grow *p.5*
The Spanish–American Empire *p.6*
The Spanish–American revolutions *p.8*
America for the Americans *p.11*
Latin America in the nineteenth century *p.11*

2 Britannia's daughters *p.15*
Canada: the first dominion *p.16*
Australia: convicts and colonists to commonwealth *p.21*
New Zealand: the new British Isles *p.26*
South Africa: Boers, British and Bantus *p.27*

3 Opening the Orient *p.31*
India: the making of the British Raj *p.31*
China: the collapse of a civilisation *p.39*
Japan: a nation transformed *p.45*

4 The Western giant *p.51*
The U.S.A. grasps her destiny *p.51*
The American Civil War *p.55*
Filling the west *p.61*
The land of opportunity *p.63*

5 The Eastern giant *p.70*
The exploration of Siberia *p.70*
The Russian Empire in Asia *p.74*

6 Partitioning Africa *p.78*
France overseas *p.78*
The dark continent *p.80*
The scramble for Africa *p.84*

7 The white man's world *p.91*

1 Republics of the New World

Fall or rise?

In 1783 Britain had to admit that her empire had failed. True, she still held many valuable colonies, but the thirteen colonies on the Atlantic coast of North America were lost. What was more, they had not been seized by some rival European power, even though Britain's old rivals, France and Spain, had played a decisive part in the fighting. The thirteen colonies had demanded their independence, and were now a federal republic called the United States of America.

What did this mean? Was it the beginning of the end for the European overseas empires that had been growing since the great age of discoveries in the fifteenth and sixteenth centuries? Must all European colonies soon break their ties with the mother country? Perhaps, in the long run, European powers must recognise that their empires would fall away from them.

But there was another way of looking at what had happened. It could be seen as an expansion of Europe, the creation of a new European state which was none the less European for being on the other side of an ocean. Americans might claim that they had a more free and independent way of life that made them different from (and superior to) the peoples who remained in Europe, but there was no denying that they themselves were Europeans in all essentials: blood, tradition, language, religion. They certainly did not belong to any of the other races or cultures of mankind. They felt no kinship with the native Americans, the Red Indians, nor with the black people whom they imported from Africa to be their slaves.

So it may be much more valid to think of 1783 not as the fall of the first British Empire, but as a decisive rise in European influence in the world. A new European nation had been created far beyond the old geographical limits of Europe.

right: *The Red Indian chief Thayendanegea, or Joseph Brant, a friend of the Prince of Wales, has the air of an eighteenth-century gentleman in his portrait by Wilhelm von M. Berczy.*

far right: *Thomas Jefferson, 'founding father' of the United States of America, was a distinguished example of eighteenth-century European culture. This is Monticello, his home in Virginia.*

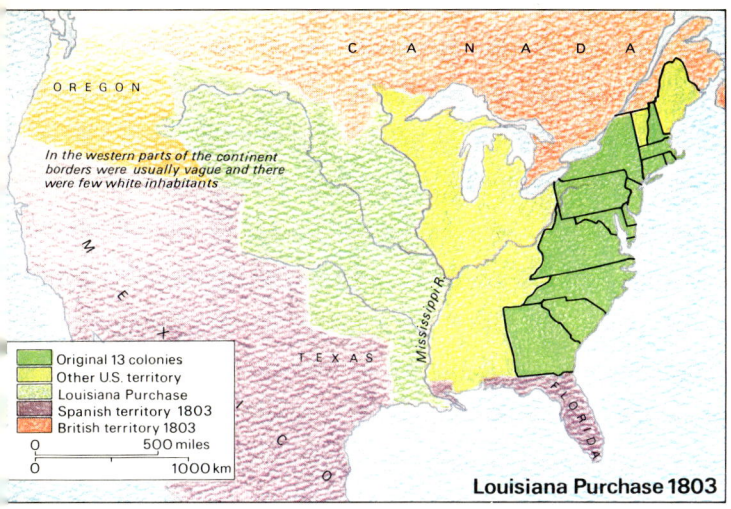

The first cotton gin – the scene as imagined by an artist many years later. The revolving cylinders with metal cat-like claws stripped the seeds from the fibres fifty times as fast as a slave could do the job by hand.

The U.S.A. begins to grow

Whatever their cultural inheritance, the leaders of the new republic were determined not to get involved in European politics, in what they saw as useless squabbles where kings wasted their peoples' lives and money. But the U.S.A. could not do as Japan had once done, cut herself off from the outside world. The Americans needed to trade with Europe, and this meant that they had to have ambassadors at the European courts.

The U.S.A. had hardly settled its own constitution when Europe plunged into the long, complicated wars of the French Revolution and Napoleon. The U.S.A. soon needed a navy to protect her merchant ships, and fought France from 1798 to 1801 and Britain from 1812 to 1814 because of their interference with U.S. ships. There was also trouble with the pirate cities of Algiers, Tunis and Tripoli. None of these wars settled anything.

Yet indirectly the Napoleonic Wars brought about a huge change on the North American continent itself. The U.S.A. bought 828,000 square miles of land in what has become famous as the biggest land deal in history, the Louisiana Purchase. At this time the name Louisiana covered the whole area drained by the Mississippi and its tributaries, the heart of the North American continent. It had been claimed by both Spain and France, but Napoleon had made Spain give it to him in 1800. (Probably such treaty changes made almost as little practical difference to the scattered white inhabitants as they did to the Indians of the prairie.) Soon Napoleon decided that he had no use for an American empire, so he might as well make a profit in cash. In 1803 President Jefferson gave him 15 million dollars for it, and doubled the size of the U.S.A.

Meanwhile there were signs that Americans were inventive and enterprising enough to develop an industrial revolution like the one that had begun in Britain. Robert Fulton, having failed to interest Napoleon in steamships and underwater warfare, returned home and had his steamer *Clermont* plying on the Hudson River by 1807. Eli Whitney did even more to shape the future. He invented the cotton gin, which made it far easier to strip the fibres from the cotton plant, and so caused a very big increase in the slave-operated cotton plantations of the southern states. A few years later he set up a factory for making muskets, where each workman did only one special job and then passed on the musket to the next man. Some have seen this as the first production line, the beginning of a system of mass production.

The Spanish–American Empire

The Spanish Empire made other European colonies in the New World look poor and primitive. It was vast, and the original two viceroyalties had had to be increased in the eighteenth century as the white population grew and the Spanish government tried to govern more closely. The officials were mostly Spaniards from Spain, *peninsulares* as they were called, whom the king thought that he could trust to carry out his orders better than Spaniards born in America, who were known as *criollos* or creoles.

Creoles and peninsulares distrusted each other. Many of the creoles were wealthy and highly educated, and the cultivated, fashionable society of cities like Lima and Mexico was at least as elegant as that of most European capitals. Some creoles were keen readers of books by Enlightened French writers and shared the ideas of Rousseau and Voltaire, and some had travelled in Europe. Such men often resented being ruled so completely from Spain, and thought seriously about the example set by the thirteen British colonies to the north. But South America was simply too big to become a copy of the U.S.A. The creoles thought of themselves as being Americans as well as Spaniards, but even more they were coming to think of themselves as Mexicans, or Venezuelans or Chileans.

The government also had taken up many of the ideas of the Enlightenment, and one of these was to free trade from old mercantile restrictions which had tied the colonists to trading only with Spain. But this was not such a boon to the creoles as it seemed to be. The people who did best out of the reforms were merchants in Spain. It was true that the South American farmers, planters and ranchers now had more freedom to sell their produce – grain, sugar, coffee, meat, hides, indigo – and they profited. But on the other hand European manufactured goods could be bought more easily, and this competition was a severe blow to the creoles who were trying to set up industries in South America, like cloth in Mexico and iron in La Plata. Thus the creoles were further divided by their attitudes to the economic situation.

So far it may have seemed as though the creoles were the only people in Spanish America. They were certainly the most important, the undoubted leaders in every way. But numerically they were only a small minority of the total population. The South American population was probably the greatest racial mixture in the world. There were the three basic races: native Indians, European colonists and African slaves. These had intermarried over more than two centuries and had produced an incredibly complicated range of colours and faces. Roughly, a person's position in society depended on the amount of white blood – that is, blood of the conquerors and rulers – in his veins. Sometimes there were laws to keep the lower grades down; mulattos (mixed white–black) in Venezuela, for example, could not dress like whites, marry whites, obtain higher education, become priests, officials or soldiers. But towards the end of the eighteenth century the Spanish government began to insist that such restrictions be abolished.

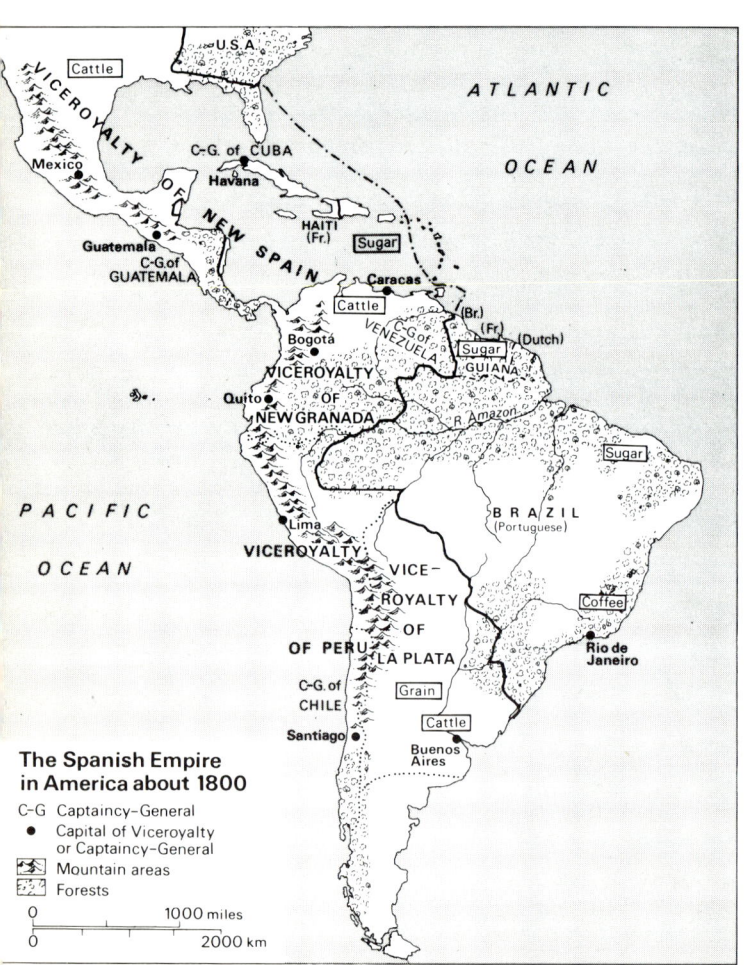

The Spanish Empire in America about 1800

C-G Captaincy-General
• Capital of Viceroyalty or Captaincy-General
Mountain areas
Forests

Now the lower castes, if they had the brains and determination, could rise to important positions.

In some places the creoles were appalled. In Mexico and Peru, where there were large settled Indian populations, and in Venezuela and Cuba, where many Africans had been imported for the plantations, whites feared that any relaxation would encourage revolts and massacres. (This was not mere imagination; it had happened in the French colony of Haiti in 1793 when revolutionary ideas spread among the blacks.) In other places, like Chile and La Plata, where there were relatively few settled Indians or negroes, though there was constant fighting with the unconquered Indians of the southern frontiers, the creoles did not have the same fears.

The Spanish Empire in America, about 1800, presented a picture of enormous variety: different countries, climates, peoples. Distances were great and transport slow. The Spanish government had succeeded in imposing unity of a sort on the continent: the same official language, the same system of law and administration, the same Church. This did not prevent a great deal of disagreement and discontent, but there was as much ill-feeling between the colonial people themselves as against the government in Spain. One thing about the government's reforms did indeed annoy everybody. They cost money, and so the taxes were increased. This led to a few risings, but these never grew into anything like a revolution. Instead, they may even have made revolution less likely, if they alarmed the creoles. Rather than risk the unknown violence of the lower castes bursting loose, they would go on putting up with the government in Madrid.

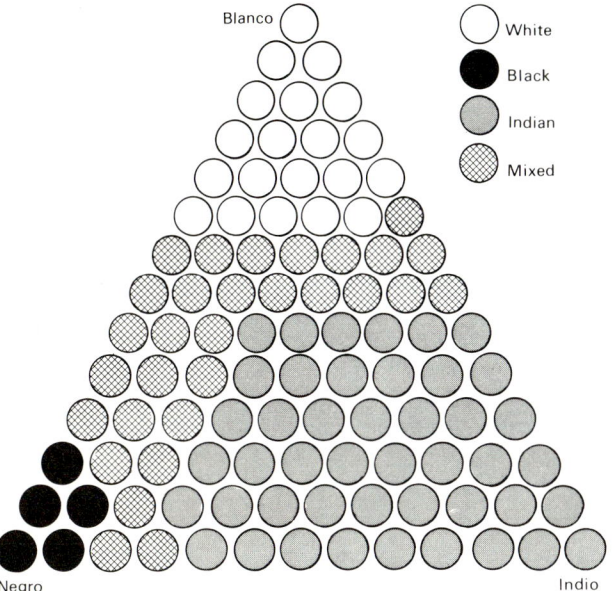

Racial mixtures in Spanish America, about 1800

Blanco / Negro / Indio

White / Black / Indian / Mixed

The names on the pyramid are the Spanish versions of the three main 'pure' races. The three main 'mixtures' were: mulato (blanco and negro); mestizo (blanco and indio); zambo (indio and negro). There were all sorts of other proportions of mixed blood possible. The diagram shows approximate proportions; the exact numbers are not known.

The owner of a Mexican hacienda (estate), dressed in fashionable European style, with some Spanish and Mexican variations. This print, like those on the following pages, is from a series on Mexican costume published by C. Linati in Brussels, early in the nineteenth century.

The Spanish–American revolutions

There was no serious trouble until Spain herself collapsed in the Napoleonic Wars. The first sign came when Spain was an unwilling ally of France, and therefore Britain attacked Spanish colonies. Since Britain's navy controlled the seas, there could be no help from Spain. In 1806 and 1807 British forces twice tried to take Buenos Aires. Both times they were soundly beaten – but not by regular Spanish troops. Local forces won the victory. The colonials had been left to rely on their own strength for protection and had proved that they could succeed.

In 1808 Napoleon invaded Spain after trapping and imprisoning the royal family. It was the beginning of a confused and savage struggle, with the British now helping the Spaniards. It was hard to be sure who legally ruled Spain, though a central *junta* (committee) was set up to carry on until the king could return. There were also local juntas in the various provinces. Was the Spanish national junta entitled to rule the empire too? In Spanish America it seemed to many of the leading creoles that they had as much right as the Spaniards to set up committees until the king was restored. By 1810 there were juntas in La Paz (the chief city of Upper Peru), Santiago (Chile), Bogotá (New Granada), Caracas (Venezuela) and Buenos Aires (La Plata). Each claimed to control its province in the name of the king.

The chief Spanish official in South America was the Viceroy of Peru, with his capital at Lima. He would not recognise the juntas. He knew that the men leading them were not revolutionaries, but he also believed that once they had tasted power they would not want to go back to obeying orders from Spain. When the juntas refused to resign he set about putting them down by force.

Once fighting began, people had to take sides. Many were very reluctant, but there were some who saw this as the opportunity they had been waiting for. These were the genuine revolutionaries, men who already sincerely believed that South America should be independent and republican. But the viceroy's troops won, and by 1815, when Napoleon had fallen and the king once more ruled in Spain, he had regained control everywhere except in La Plata. It seemed that the revolution, if it could be called such, was over. Perhaps it would have been, but for the efforts of two revolutionary leaders: Simón Bolívar and José de San Martín.

Bolívar was a wealthy young Venezuelan who had travelled in Europe and become passionately convinced that revolution was right. Fighting against the viceroy's forces he was often put to flight, but he always came back. He managed to persuade all sorts of people to help him, from the savage *llaneros*, cowboys of the plains who fought for pleasure and loot, to disciplined British ex-regulars, who fought for pay. He became an expert guerrilla leader, knowing how, with small forces, to keep a whole country alarmed and uncertain. He also knew the value of ambitious propaganda; in 1819, while still very weak, he proclaimed the Republic of Great Colombia, covering all the territories of Venezuela and New

Granada. Even when he was not winning, he tried to make everybody believe that he was.

At this stage it was San Martín who really turned the tide by winning solid military victories. He was an ex-officer of the Spanish army, though born in La Plata, and he understood that there could be no patched-up agreement now. It would have to be complete victory or defeat over the whole continent. The royalist forces would have to be attacked and destroyed in their stronghold of Peru. It was a bold idea, but San Martín was no fool. He knew that the difficulties of marching direct from La Plata to Peru were too great. He must find a new base.

The two great liberators in their Napoleonic-style uniforms, both painted by José Gil de Castro: Simón Bolívar, 1783–1820, painted in Lima, 1825 (left) and José de San Martín, 1778–1850, painted after the battle of Chacabuco, 1817.

More Mexican types drawn by Linati. The fashionably dressed lady indulges her religious tastes by dressing her little son as a friar. The peasant girl is an Indian from Tehuantepec in the south and stands near the cactus from which her people get fibre for making cloth and juice for making strong drink. The beggar is carrying the crippled woman by means of a tumpline.

He took Chile. Here there was a revolutionary group led by Bernardo O'Higgins, son of an Irishman who had served Spain and become Viceroy of Peru in the 1790s. San Martín made a surprise march over the Andes and won the battle of Chacabuco in 1817. A year later Chile was proclaimed an independent republic with O'Higgins as Supreme Director, and San Martín planned to invade Peru. For this he wanted sea power, and he employed Lord Cochrane, a brilliant but temperamental British naval officer. Cochrane won control of the sea and in 1820 landed San Martín and his army on the coast of Peru, within striking distance of Lima.

1820 was the year of decision. But again it depended more on events in Europe than South America. There was a revolution in Spain itself and liberals took over the government. Would they come to terms with fellow-revolutionaries in America? There were truces and talks. Eventually the wars went on, because even the liberals in Spain had no wish to lose their empire. But by now the royalists in South America had had their confidence shaken. If Spain herself was not really dependable, what were they fighting for?

Now it was Bolívar's turn. In 1821 he won the battle of Carabobo, and royalist resistance in Venezuela collapsed. Meanwhile his lieutenant Sucre siezed the area around Quito, and the Republic of Great Colombia became a reality.

The situation had now turned dramatically against the royalists. Peru was being invaded by Bolívar's men from the north, San Martín's from the west. But there was still hope. The two great revolutionary leaders might easily quarrel; Bolívar was notoriously ambitious and intolerant. San Martín and Bolívar met at Guayaquil, and the future of the revolution hung on whether or not they could agree. San Martín soon saw that he could not work with Bolívar. But he was not ambitious and he wanted the revolution to succeed. So he retired, and left it to Bolívar and Sucre to finish the war. They destroyed the last royalists at the battles of Junín and Ayacucho. When the revolutionaries proclaimed a republic in Upper Peru they named it Bolivia, and renamed one of its chief towns Sucre.

North of the Isthmus of Panama the revolution took a very different shape; events in South America seemed to have little influence in Central America. Here everything depended on what happened in Mexico, and in Mexico the royalists remained in control. The reason was that here there had been a revolutionary upheaval *amongst the Indians*, and the creoles had learnt their lesson. It had happened in 1810, when Miguel Hidalgo, parish priest of the small town of Dolores, became the leader of one of the local junta-type secret societies that were fashionable at the time and turned it into a massive Indian uprising. He demanded an end to the special tax that Indian peasants paid, and that land be distributed afresh to the peasants. Perhaps as many as 80,000 gathered behind him, a huge uncontrollable mob that swept through the countryside

More Linati drawings.
The Friar setting off on a journey is equipped like any other rider in rough country, and his horse wears leather protectors against cactus and thorns. Liberals often accused the clergy of enjoying riches while the poor starved, though in fact the wealth of the Church was mainly controlled by the government, both before and after the revolution.

The revolutionary priest Hidalgo: this portrait is probably based on descriptions by other people and on what the artist himself knew about the dress of Mexican priests.

killing all Spaniards and many creoles. They were a terror to peaceful people, but soon 6,000 soldiers routed them, and Hidalgo was caught and executed. However, in another area another priest, José María Morelos, took up the cause; he became a clever guerrilla leader, and was not caught and killed until 1815. The dreaded revolt of the lowest castes had come near enough to make the Mexican upper classes cling for protection to the Spanish government.

1820 changed the situation. The new liberal government in Spain seemed to be thinking of the sort of reform that Hidalgo and Morelos had wanted. The only way of stopping this seemed to be to break away from Spain, and in 1821 some leading Mexicans declared independence. Next year a soldier named Agustín de Iturbide made himself Emperor of Mexico. It was not revolution, but fear of it that had led to this.

The smaller provinces of Central America remained fairly quiet and simply went along with Mexico. But in 1823 Iturbide fell and Mexico became a federal republic, on the U.S.A. pattern. At this the smaller states decided that they would be better off in a federation of their own, and Guatemala, Salvador, Nicaragua, Honduras and Costa Rica formed the United Provinces of Central America.

By the middle 1820s the islands of Cuba and Puerto Rico were all that remained of the Spanish–American Empire, providing a refuge for royalists fleeing from the new republics of the mainland.

One very large part of South America had never belonged to Spain. Brazil was Portuguese. Brazil declared her independence also, but in a remarkably different way. During the Peninsular War the Portuguese royal family had fled to Brazil when the French invaded their country. The king liked it so well that he remained there after the defeat of Napoleon. He did not return to Portugal until 1820, when the new liberal government (there had been a revolution in Portugal as well as in Spain) said that it needed him. He left his son to look after Brazil. The Portuguese government soon made it clear that Brazil was not to enjoy a privileged position in the Portuguese Empire any longer. Leading Brazilians, though, were determined to keep the advantages that went with having a royal court in their country. So they simply declared Brazil an independent empire, with the prince as emperor. Not a shot was fired.

America for the Americans

Almost the whole continent was now liberated – though there could be a lot of argument about what that word really meant. The Spanish–American revolutionaries had fought hard, but they had received help, especially from Britain. In 1823, with the rather luke-warm approval of other European powers, France sent troops to help to overthrow the liberal government in Spain and restore the king to his old authority. The next step was going to be to help the king to retake Spanish America. But the British government let it be known that the Royal Navy would be ordered to intercept any such expeditions, and that was the end of the matter.

Why did Britain do this? One explanation was that the British believed in liberty for all peoples, and this was certainly a strong motive in men like Cochrane. But Britain was also the home of the Industrial Revolution, and her businessmen wanted to be able to sell manufactures – cloth and hardware, for example – and to buy South American produce without interference from Spain. The trade was prospering and Britain needed it to help her industries through the difficult years after the end of the Napoleonic Wars, and this was probably the main reason in the thinking of the government.

In December 1823 the U.S.A. also intervened. President Monroe declared that if any European state tried to extend its rule over any part of the American continent the U.S.A. would regard this as a threat to peace. In other words, the U.S.A. was now the self-appointed guardian of all the Americas against European interference. This became known as the Monroe Doctrine. At the time Monroe's words were only words; the U.S.A. was far too weak to fight a major war, and the British navy had already ensured that there would be no war. But as the U.S.A. and the other American republics grew during the nineteenth century the Monroe Doctrine also grew and became important.

Latin America in the nineteenth century

The boundaries of the new republics were settled fairly soon. Great Colombia split up in 1830, forming three separate republics: Colombia, Ecuador and Venezuela. Uruguay fought for independence from her bigger neighbours, Brazil and Argentina, and won. (Argentina was the name by which the old provinces of La Plata were now known.) After this, the frontiers did not change much. The only serious alteration was in 1889, when Chile defeated Peru and Bolivia, and seized Bolivia's entire coast; it was desert, but it was rich in nitrates, and by this time European farmers were buying nitrates as fertilisers.

Some countries changed their constitutions. There were bitter struggles in Argentina between those who wanted it to be a loose grouping of provinces and those who preferred a strong central government to rule the vast country. After many years of strife, the result was a fairly tight federation with Buenos Aires enjoying special rights as capital. The other giant, Brazil, became a republic in 1889 when the army deposed the emperor, and two years later it also adopted a federal form of government. It was henceforward the United States of Brazil – larger in area than the United States of America.

Compared with the upheavals in the rest of the world, including Europe, Latin America can hardly be said to have undergone extraordinary troubles. Yet South America came to have the reputation, in Europe and North America, of being a land of violence, where governments rose and fell by force and bribery, and where the wilds were infested by bandits. It was exaggerated and unfair, but not entirely untrue.

The main problem was the *caudillo*, the local strong man or boss. Once Spanish rule had gone, there was usually nothing effective to take its place. The new governments needed time to gain experience and to get people into the habit of obeying, after years of arguing and fighting. But everybody knew that governments could be unmade as quickly as they had been made. Distances were great and communications often poor, so a local leader could build up a strong following without much risk of interference from the capital. His followers could soon become an army. In many areas men always carried arms for protection against Indians and wild beasts, and were quick to use them. Cowboys like the famous *gauchos* of Argentina made first-class irregular cavalry, tough and resourceful. Even the humble Indian peasant farmer, born and bred to a life of stoical obedience, could become an infantryman of astonishing endurance and loyalty. A successful caudillo did not survive simply by speeches and promises.

Men of this type, sometimes honestly believing that they were doing what was best for their country, but always ambitious and ruthless, struggled for power in many republics. One of the most famous was Juan Manuel de Rosas, who became governor of Buenos Aires province in 1829 and ruled all Argentina from 1835 to 1852, persuading or forcing the caudillos of other provinces to work with him. He may have helped his country by enforcing some sort of order, but he was brutal and he quarrelled with other republics. The most notorious 'strong man' of all was Francisco López, who succeeded his father as president of Paraguay in 1862 and had grandiose ideas of being a great conqueror. From his small and poor state he raised the largest army in South America, and fought the combined forces of Argentina, Brazil and Uruguay.

When he was killed in 1870, five years of war had reduced the population of his country from about half a million to 221,079 (census figure of 1871) of whom only 28,746 were adult males. Rosas and López are extreme examples, but it was common in most republics for rival political factions to take up arms, and for presidents to come and go by force. So it came to seem to outsiders that there was always a revolution going on somewhere or other in South or Central America.

These republics were not poor, though most of their people were. As the populations and riches of Europe and North America increased, so those countries demanded more of the products of Latin America – coffee, sugar, red mahogany wood for Victorian furniture. New inventions increased the demand. When chemistry was applied to farming and new fertilisers were introduced, there was a demand for nitrates and phosphates. As the canning of meat improved, the ranchers of the *pampas* supplied a huge corned beef industry. All this made creole landowners and traders richer, though the poor who worked for them saw little of the extra wealth. Industries, however, did not grow. This was partly through lack of coal and iron, but mainly because the European and North American factories supplied so much that there seemed

Two of the many scenes of nineteenth-century gaucho *life painted by Juan Leon Pallière. One shows a corral on the pampa, with gauchos training horses, the other a gaucho talking to a woman who is mashing corn beside a well. What the gaucho wore was a mixture of the showy and the practical. Each 'half-foot boot' was made from the whole skin of a colt's back leg, very strong and pliable, and the huge spurs were usually of silver. Over the ornate belt was looped the simple hunting* bolas. *The gaily decorated poncho did good service as blanket, overcoat and shield.*

to be no opening for local industries to start. In fact, South America still had what is termed a colonial economy, supplying raw materials and importing manufactures, as it had done in the time of the Spanish Empire. Sometimes it even seemed as if some republics were not independent after all, because foreign businessmen (mainly British, U.S. and German) were so powerful that the government dared not offend them, especially when these businessmen could rely on the support of their own governments in times of trouble. Some small Central American states became known by the end of the century as 'the banana republics' because they were so helplessly under the influence of U.S. fruit companies.

Even if foreigners did control much of it, there was a great deal of trade. Towns grew, especially seaports and centres of the railways that foreign (mainly British) engineers were building. Into these towns poured a growing stream of immigrants, mostly from southern Europe. Buenos Aires had about 42,000 inhabitants at the beginning of the century, 177,767 in 1869 at the time of the first Argentinian census, and passed the million mark in 1905. This was the biggest city, but at the end of the century Rio de Janeiro had a population of about 750,000 and Mexico City about 400,000.

The Liebig Extract of Meat Company built its first meat-packing plant at Fray Bentos, Uruguay, in 1865; photographed about 1895 (above). The railway linking São Paulo, Brazil, to the port of Santos, built by British engineers; photographed in 1867 (below).

While all this nineteenth-century progress went on in some places, there were also vast areas that remained quite untouched by civilisation of any sort. This was especially true of the forests of the Amazon basin, which summed up this continent of contrasts. By 1900 the Amazon was a highway for ocean-going steamers, and in the heart of the jungle they came to the city of Manaus, complete with its opera house, paid for by the proceeds of the boom in rubber. At the end of the century prospectors were able to get high prices for the rubber they collected from trees in the heart of the jungle; to supply modern civilisation these men forced the primitive Indians of the forest to work for them and often treated them cruelly.

What, in fact, had the revolutions done for those millions of South Americans whom Bolívar had once called 'the oppressed classes'? The wild Indians were eventually beaten, in some places wiped out completely. The millions of settled Indians went on as before, very poor peasants. Many of them were little more than slaves, because they had borrowed money from their landlords in famine years, and could not leave until they paid off the debt, which was hardly possible for people so poor. These people were probably worse off than they had been before the revolutions, because now there was no imperial government to try to protect them. The republican governments sometimes passed impressive-sounding laws to help the poor, but usually failed to enforce them. The revolutions had liberated the creoles more than the lower castes. Sometimes, it is true, men of Indian descent became powerful. One of these was Benito Juárez, a lawyer who led the Mexican liberals and was president from 1858 to his death in 1872. It was Juárez who led the resistance when Napoleon III of France tried to create a puppet empire in Mexico, with the Austrian prince Maximilian at its head, and it was Juárez who had Maximilian shot after the French withdrew their troops. Porfirio Díaz, who ruled Mexico from 1876 to 1911, was also of Indian blood, but he did nothing for his own people. Under Díaz there were new industries, mines and railways, but they were mostly controlled by foreign businessmen. The Díaz government favoured the rich, while the poor became, if possible, poorer than ever. Mexico may be an extreme example; but it is not unfair to say that, after a century, it seemed that the people who had done well out of the revolutions in Latin America were not the poor, but the old creole families and the new immigrants from Europe.

2 Britannia's daughters

When the thirteen American colonies broke away, many British seriously questioned whether they had ever really been worth what they had cost. In the very year of the American Declaration of Independence, 1776, Adam Smith published *The Wealth of Nations*, arguing that free trade, not private empires, was what brought most prosperity, and many powerful people were convinced by his arguments. Though it was to be nearly a hundred years before Britain became a free-trade country without restrictions on imports and exports, from Smith's time onwards there was a steady movement towards free trade.

Free trade, like any other freedom, favoured the strongest. The Industrial Revolution put Britain far ahead of other countries in manufacturing and commerce, and it was only Britain's farmers and the least efficient of the manufacturers who feared free trade. We have already seen how Latin America became a very lucrative market for the goods of Birmingham, Leeds and Manchester. Provided she could enjoy this sort of freedom, why should Britain take on the trouble and expense of colonies?

But still Britain had to be strong enough to make sure that nobody tried to interfere with her traders. The seas must be open highways for peaceful merchant ships. This became the task of the Royal Navy. As a result of the Napoleonic Wars, Britain was recognised as being far and away the greatest sea power in the world, and in the peace settlement of 1815 Britain kept a number of islands and ports – Cape Town, for instance – which would be valuable supply bases for her ships.

During the nineteenth century the British navy acted as the police force of the seas. The pirates of the Red Sea and Persian Gulf, the East Indian and China Seas were reduced from fleets of bold adventurers to a few miserable sneak-thieves. The navy's work was not entirely selfish. In the early nineteenth century most European states came to see the slave trade as a monstrous cruelty that no civilised people should permit, and they outlawed it. Enforcement was another duty of the Royal Navy. In tasks like this, though warships of other nations often played a valuable part, there was never any doubt that Britannia was ruling the waves.

So Britain could prosper without any need to expand her empire, apart from a few small bases for her ships, and most British governments during the century had no desire for more. Yet it was just at this time that Britain's empire grew to an extent hardly equalled in world history, and Britain founded what soon grew into new European nations across the oceans.

The British sloop 'Primrose' capturing the Portuguese slaver 'Velos Passagero' off the West African coast, 6 September 1830. Engraved by Duncan after an oil painting by William Huggins.

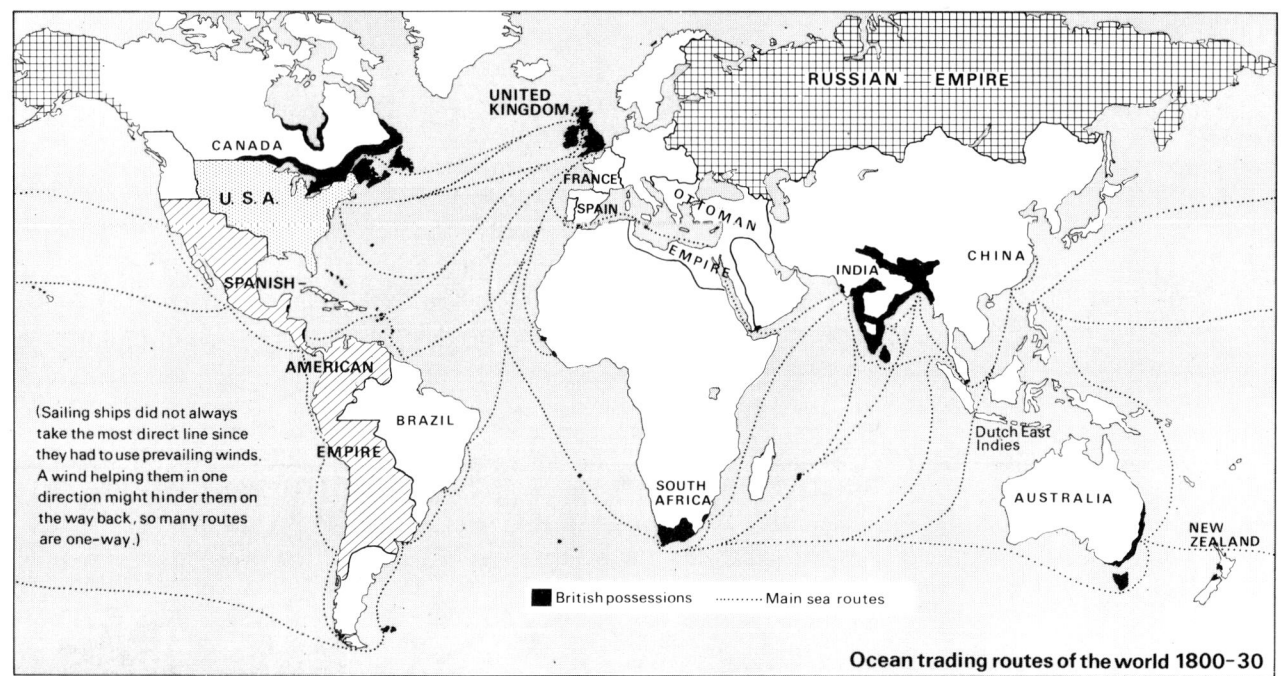

Ocean trading routes of the world 1800-30

Canada, the first dominion

Even after losing the thirteen colonies Britain had several left in North America: Newfoundland, Nova Scotia, New Brunswick, Prince Edward Island, and Canada. Canada was the odd one. The others lay on the coast and were mainly settled by English, Welsh, Scottish and Irish. Canada lay up the St Lawrence and was French. When Britain had taken Canada from France in 1763 she had promised to allow the settlers to go on using their own language, religion and laws. Britain kept her promise, and on their side the Canadians kept their promise to obey their new rulers. Then after the War of American Independence thousands of colonists who remained loyal to Britain came streaming northwards to settle on land that was still under King George. These United Empire Loyalists, as they were called, preferred to settle away from the French area, to the west. They were entirely different people and it seemed best to set up a separate colony for them. So this was called Upper Canada and the old French part was now known as Lower Canada.

These colonies had what was called *representative government*. This meant that the colonists elected representatives who formed an assembly to advise the governor, who was appointed by the British government. But they could only advise, and had no power. It was the governor who had the responsibility of ruling the colony, and he took the decisions. This system worked well enough. At any rate, when U.S. forces tried to 'liberate' Canada in the 1812 war, both British and French Canadians – and Indians – helped the small British army to drive them back.

After the Napoleonic Wars, however, attitudes began to change. The population grew, especially in Upper Canada, as thousands of people migrated from Britain in the hope of a more prosperous life and wider opportunities. As the colonists became more numerous and richer, they began to think that they were entitled to have more say in running the colony. There was disagreement among the colonists themselves. The newcomers in Upper Canada resented the way United Empire Loyalist families seemed to think that they were the only people who mattered, while the French in Lower Canada feared that they would be submerged by the waves of British immigrants. Feelings ran high. There were even a couple of

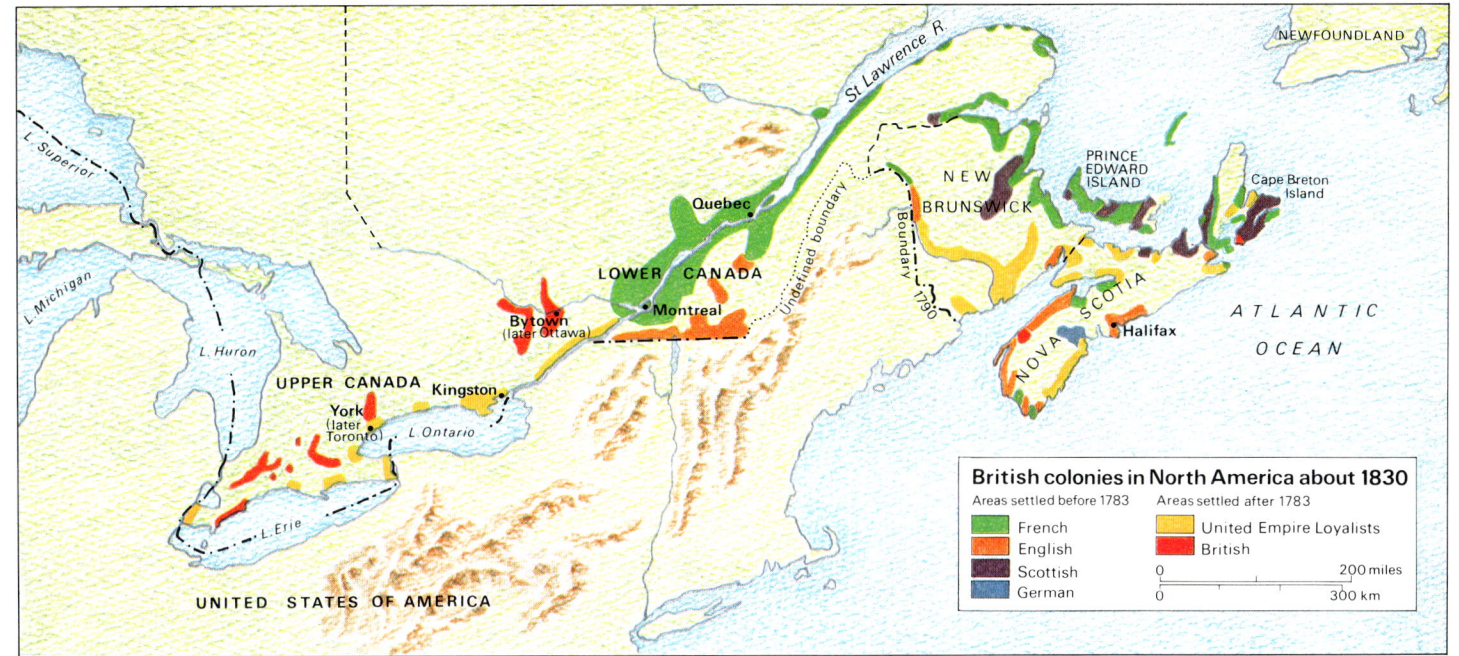

attempts at rebellion. The British government after 1832 was especially likely to take demands for reform seriously, since it had itself come to power as a result of the Parliamentary reform of 1832. So it sent Lord Durham, a man so well known for his liberal ideas that he was nicknamed 'Radical Jack', to report on what ought to be done.

The Durham Report of 1839 was clear and definite. It said that some Canadians were merely troublemakers, but that on the whole the Canadians ought to be given the responsibility of ruling themselves in all internal matters except control of unsettled land and of tariffs. The two Canadas should also be united. Thus, with serious work to do, those Canadians who were interested in politics could act together to build up the country instead of wasting their energy on quarrels which could only lead to a complete breakdown of colonial government.

The British government had not been prepared for anything quite so sweeping, but by the Canada Union Act of 1840 both provinces were brought together under one governor and given one assembly in which Upper and Lower Canada had an equal number of members. The assembly was not given extra powers; this was still only representative government. But in fact the governor from now on acted only with the agreement of the leaders of the assembly, so that the province really had what amounted to *responsible* government.

Despite this, bad feeling continued. The French and British parts still distrusted each other. Some Canadians therefore suggested that the best solution might be a federal system, rather like the U.S.A., with each part having guaranteed rights. By now it was the 1860s, and the U.S.A. was being torn by a civil war that had arisen largely because the U.S. constitution had not made clear whether final authority lay with the individual states or with the federal government. Warned by this, the Canadians suggested that all powers that were not clearly written down as belonging to the provinces would belong to the central government. One of the advantages of the federal idea was that other provinces could join. Nova Scotia, New Brunswick and Prince Edward Island were interested, and there were wide lands to the west which might well become new provinces in the future.

The British government accepted these suggestions, and in 1867 the British North America Act was passed, creating the

Dominion of Canada, with a federal capital at Ottawa. The name 'dominion' was chosen as something that was new, that would not seem to carry associations with any disputes in the past.

The system worked. The people of the dominion governed themselves in their provinces and also in the federal government; so in most ways they were as good as independent. At the same time they remained members of the British Empire, which gave them protection and strength, as well as keeping the emotional links with the mother country. This was to be an example for other British colonies. It proved that it was possible for colonies to grow to independence without breaking away from the empire that had founded them, and *dominion status* became something that other British colonies could obtain when they were big enough.

We have followed the story of the development of the dominion idea in the eastern part of British North America, and this was where almost all the white inhabitants lived. But on the western side of the continent a colony was by now growing rapidly in British Columbia. Here was an area that had been claimed for Britain by Captain Vancouver and where fur traders had set up posts in the 1790s. Spanish explorers from California, Russian explorers from Siberia and Alaska, and U.S. explorers striking west from the Louisiana Purchase lands all reached the area in the late eighteenth century and early nineteenth, and there were sometimes fierce arguments between rival fur traders. The governments, however, did not think that it was worth while to fight over this remote land, and eventually the frontiers were agreed peacefully.

There was an enormous area between Canada and British Columbia, stretching far to the north. Much of it was forest land where travel was difficult except by river. It was inhabited by Indians, though not very many – most preferred to live further south – and animals with splendid fur coats. To trap them was a hard but very profitable business, and trappers from French Canada and the British Hudson Bay Company had roamed this vast wilderness since the late seventeenth century, living like the Indians and trading with them. Many of the immigrants to Canada in the later eighteenth century were Scottish Highlanders who left their homes after the failure of the Jacobite risings or because their landlords turned them out in order to pasture sheep on their crofts. It was a Scot, Alexan-

The numbers of salmon in the waters of British Columbia made it possible to set up a big canning industry. 'The Salmon Harvest' by J. H. Chapman was taken about 1900; it was necessary to import workers from Japan to solder cans, as the second photograph, taken about 1913, shows.

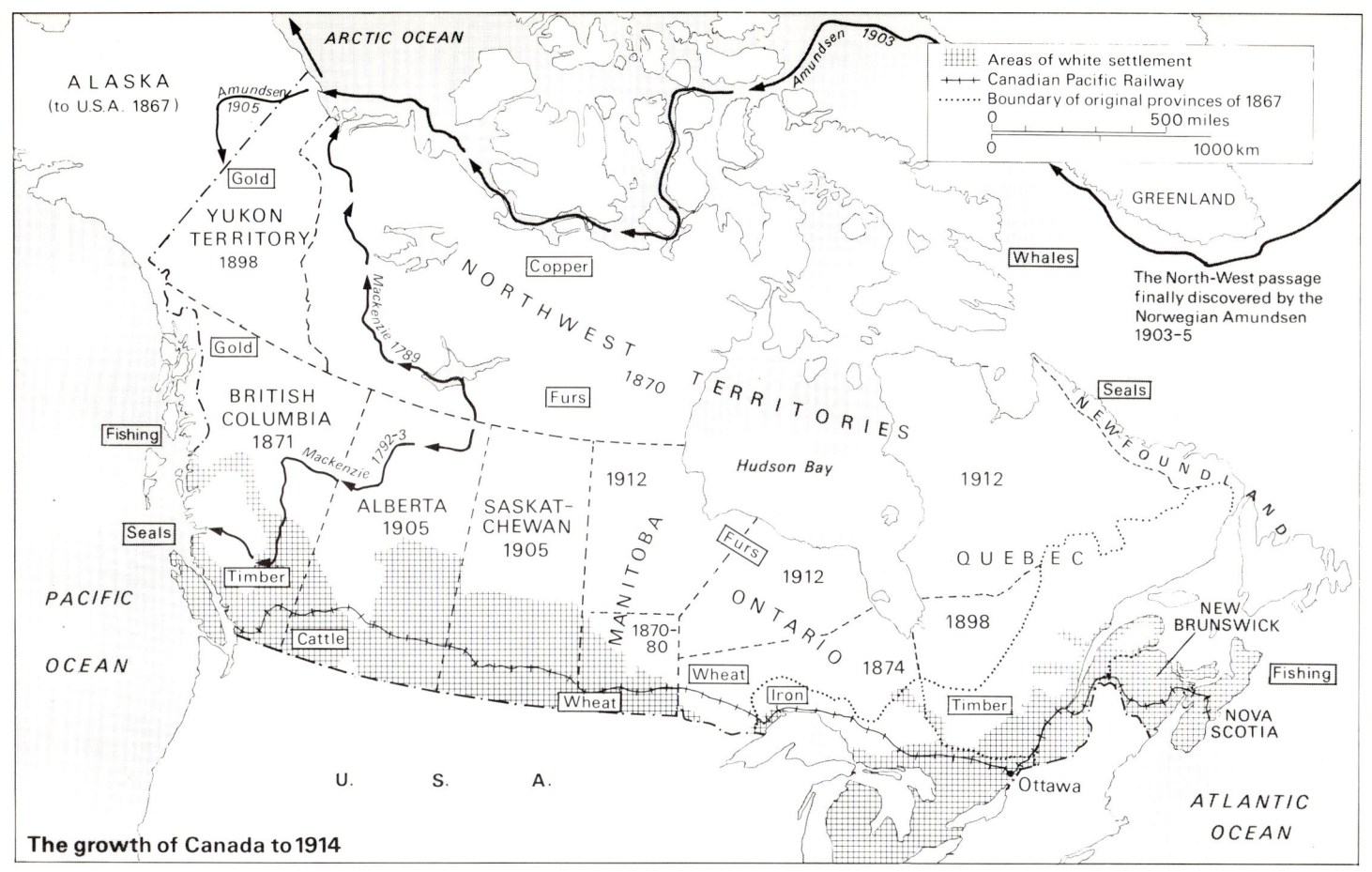

The growth of Canada to 1914

der Mackenzie, working for a fur company, who became the great explorer of the Canadian North-West. In 1789 he followed the river that now bears his name until he reached the Arctic Ocean, and four years later he found a way through the Rocky Mountains to the Pacific. In 1821 rival fur companies agreed to combine to form a new Hudson Bay Company which was recognised by the British government as having a monopoly over the whole North-West. This certainly stopped fights, but it did not encourage new settlers and traders.

While the northern parts remained mainly the preserves of the trappers, the plains further south slowly began to be occupied. Some of this land proved good for cattle ranching and some of it for growing wheat. The border with the U.S.A. had been agreed along the parallel of 49 degrees latitude by treaties in 1818 and 1846, when it seemed that there was plenty of space for everybody, and these treaties were respected. There was not much trouble with the Red Indians, either. This was probably because the tribes were not very numerous and the white men came much more slowly and quietly than further south, in the U.S.A. Perhaps credit should also be given to the North-West Mounted Police (later the Royal Canadian Mounted Police) who earned a great reputation for keeping law and order with only the minimum force. Apart from suppressing a couple of small rebellions stirred up by French–Canadian half-breeds the soldiers stationed in Canada were not needed.

The modern colour photographs give a vivid impression of the flat farmlands of central Canada, linked to their markets by the railway, and of the forested mountains of British Columbia, criss-crossed by tracks for the foresters and lumberjacks. The older photograph shows work at a logging camp in Manitoba in the 1890s.

So the history of the Dominion of Canada during the later nineteenth century was one of peaceful growth and prosperity. When the Canadian Pacific Railway was completed in 1885 it became easier for settlers to move in and for corn and meat to be exported. So the gap between old Canada and the Pacific was gradually filled with new provinces. It was a remarkable contrast with the turbulent history of South and Central America, yet there was a similarity in one respect. Canada also had a colonial-style economy. Her prosperity depended on selling her natural products to industrial countries and buying manufactures from them.

Australia: convicts and colonists to commonwealth

At first nobody wanted Australia. The Spanish and Dutch captains who sighted parts of its coasts in the seventeenth century saw nothing to suggest that there was any likelihood of rich trade. They were not even sure if it was all one big island or a group of smaller ones. In 1770 Captain James Cook touched on a part of the east coast which seemed pleasant and fertile, and he named it New South Wales; part of it had such luxuriant plants that he called it Botany Bay. But interest remained slight.

The loss of the thirteen American colonies changed the attitude of the British government. Previously it had been possible to send convicted criminals to serve their sentences of hard labour by working as slaves on plantations. After the sentence was finished, it was hoped, they would become useful colonists. At any rate, it was not likely that Britain would be troubled with them again. New South Wales sounded as if it could be a substitute for America in this respect. The government also reflected that there was always the possibility of some trade, and that it might be useful to have a base there for ships; it was spurred on when it heard that French explorers were in the Pacific and might claim Australia first. So in 1787 Captain Arthur Philip, R.N., sailed for Botany Bay. There were about 1,100 people on his ships, and 750 of these were convicts, including some women.

Philip arrived on 18 January 1788, found Botany Bay unsuitable and on 26 January moved to an excellent harbour nearby, which he named Sydney, after the minister for colonies. He claimed the whole eastern coastline of Australia for Britain and, whatever the government intended, he and his officers seem to have had ambitious ideas about beginning a great empire here. But the first few years were grim.

Animals, plants and seeds brought from Britain and other places on the way to Australia did not flourish at first in the strange land. Eventually they acclimatised, but meanwhile food was scarce. The convict-colonists were mostly unskilled in agriculture, and many of them were work-shy and vicious. Successive governors and their soldiers kept order by simple brute force. Critics of the scheme were arguing that it should be abandoned as late as 1815, but the need for somewhere to send misfits from the growing population of Britain was

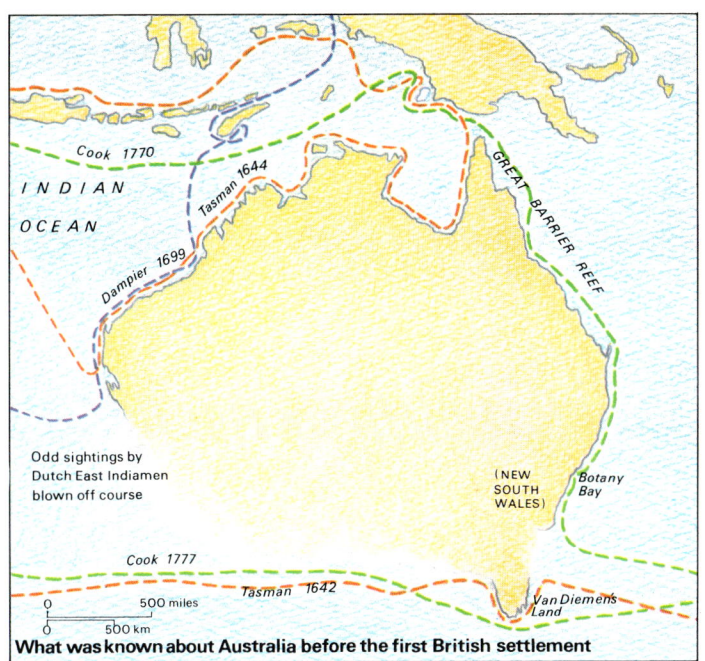

What was known about Australia before the first British settlement

strong. Instead, new settlements were founded in more remote places for particularly troublesome convicts. (There was also an idea of seeking new land to provide more varied crops, and a desire to forestall French expeditions – the old fear!) Van Diemen's Land, where the first settlement was established in 1801, became particularly notorious. A new problem soon arose, that of escaped prisoners. These men had no way of getting away from Australia, so they lived as outlaws in the wild country. They were known as bushrangers and were feared as merciless robbers and killers.

It was not likely that a great empire would grow from such beginnings, but the situation began to change when free settlers arrived. Captain John Macarthur managed to breed a strain of sheep that throve on the pastures of New South Wales and produced excellent wool. Land was there for the taking, and here was the chance of good profits. So settlers began to come, several of them people with some wealth who could afford to set up large farms. Some of the garrison officers and colonial officials, and even some enterprising ex-prisoners, also managed to earn enough money to invest in farming. The colony had been cut off from the interior of Australia by the

This water-colour shows the new road at King's Table Land in the Blue Mountains of New South Wales. The artist – Augustus Earle, 1793–1838 – has managed to convey the sense of wide lands stretching far beyond the mountains, waiting to be explored.

right: *These two commemorative stamps of 1934 sum up the swift development of Australia. The merino sheep provided the wool which first supported trade and industry. Within a century great modern cities were standing where aborigines had wandered, gathering food and hunting like the people of the Old Stone Age.*

ridge of the Blue Mountains, but passes were found in 1813; beyond were great rivers flowing westwards and vast lands wonderfully suited to grazing. Big flocks and herds, needing only a few drovers to look after them, began to move inland. From this there grew eventually the huge cattle and sheep stations which covered much of the centre of Australia.

After 1815 Australia, like Canada, received a growing number of settlers. Societies were formed in Britain to help respectable families to migrate to what seemed to be a land full of opportunities to make a better, healthier living than in British industrial towns. Most of these people naturally arrived in New South Wales, but soon settlers spread to areas far from Sydney. As their population grew, the people of these areas found it inconvenient to be governed from Sydney. To

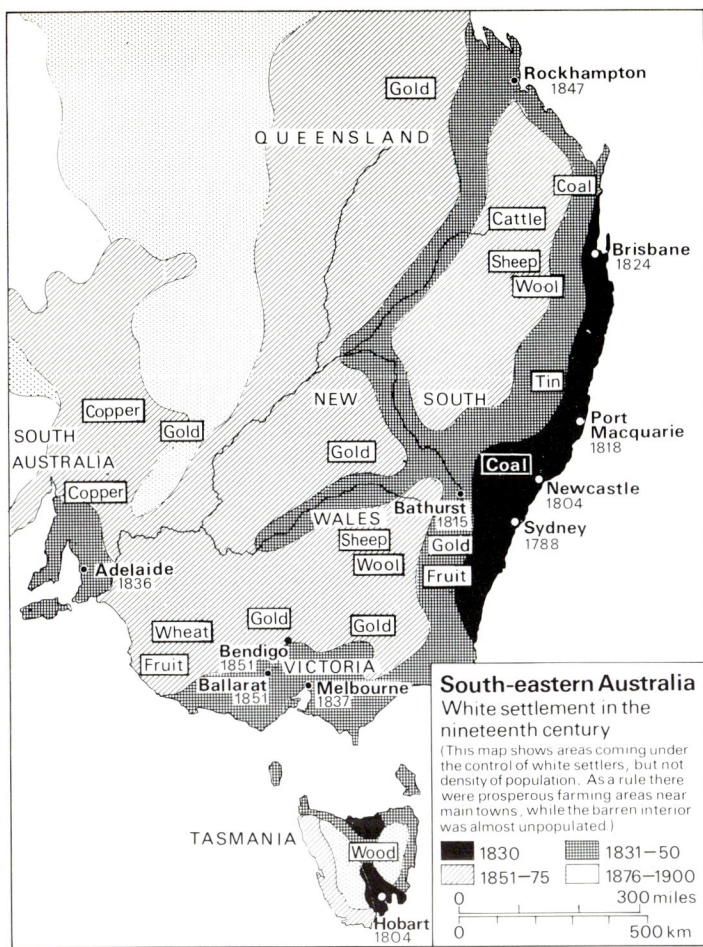

ren until it was reported that the land near Swan River was very fertile. The British government had claimed all this area of Australia, partly to prevent other European states from doing so, and was willing to sell great tracts of land very cheaply. A colonising society in Britain organised the settlement. In 1829 an advance party sailed to lay out Fremantle and Perth, and next year the main body of 4,000 arrived. The preparations had been too hurried, though, and the leaders had too little experience. Most of the colonists found their farms too big and too far apart for them to manage, and moved on to other settlements. The few who stayed had a long, hard struggle, and Western Australia was the slowest of all the colonies to grow.

Learning from this near-disaster, the people who founded a colony in South Australia were cautious. They sold the land at higher prices, partly to make sure that the colonists would think and work, and partly to gain money with which to buy more land from the government. Adelaide, named after the queen, was laid out in 1836, but the farm land was only gradually surveyed and peopled over the next few years. This cautious start was successful, in addition copper was discovered, and from about 1842 South Australia proved to be a flourishing, growing colony.

By this time the free colonists formed a great majority of the settlers, and most of them objected to criminals being still transported to live among them, though some of the wealthier wanted convicts as cheap labour. British leaders, too, now saw Australia as something very different from the human refuse dump that it had once been, and they were also influenced by penal reformers who argued that transportation did no good. The shipments of convicts were stopped in colony after colony, beginning with New South Wales in 1840. When in 1853 Van Diemen's Land ended its notorious convict history the island changed its name to Tasmania (after the Dutch discoverer who had in fact given it its old name) as a sign of the break with its past. Only Western Australia, short of labour, still was willing to accept convicts, and here the transportations did not end until 1868. After this, nothing remained of the miserable first stage of Australian settlement.

By the middle of the century the main pattern of towns and territorial divisions was becoming clear, and this naturally fitted in with the pattern of economic life. Australia was developing as an important pastoral country. In the interior,

the south the Port Philip district, a very fertile area, was settled in the 1830s, and Melbourne, named after the British Prime Minister, was founded in 1837. This grew rapidly, and the new colony was separated from New South Wales in 1851 under the name of Victoria. To the north, sheep- and cattle-owners settled from the 1830s onwards in what became the separate colony of Queensland in 1859. Van Diemen's Land had been governed separately since 1824.

While the original colony was expanding thus, other parts of Australia were being settled direct from Britain. The whole western part of the continent was empty and apparently barthe 'outback', except where the deserts were too barren, sheep grazed in their thousands and millions. They belonged to men who, claiming that the land had not belonged to anybody, 'squatted' on vast tracts where a few riders could tend thousands of sheep. These squatters often became very wealthy by selling wool, but the wool had to be taken to ports and shipped, and so this prosperous trade helped the coastal towns, which had been the first centres of settlement in Australia, to expand into bustling commercial centres. Near these towns the fertile land was filling up with farms that produced food for the growing urban populations.

In the 1850s another occupation became associated with Australian life – mining. Nearly forty years before, coal had been found at a place about 100 miles north of Sydney which was promptly named Newcastle, and copper had helped to establish the early prosperity of South Australia. The new discovery was a different kind of mineral – one that could be guaranteed to bring swarms of adventurers to dig: gold. In 1851 a veteran of the 1849 gold rush in California recognised gold-bearing rocks near Bathurst, New South Wales. Soon afterwards an even more promising area was found in Victoria, at Ballarat. Diggers came rushing, and a few became rich. One main result, when the excitement died down, was to give Australia a much stronger new industry, as some gold mines went on producing and as new minerals were found and exploited. Another result may have been to strengthen ideas of freedom and equality among the Australian colonists, because the miners resisted when the authorities attempted to treat them worse than ordinary settlers, and their stand won a lot of sympathy.

The Australian colonies were growing at such a rate that they soon wanted self-government. The British government, with the example of Canada in mind, readily agreed, even suggesting that the colonies ought themselves to frame their own constitutions. New South Wales, Tasmania, Victoria and South Australia all got responsible government in 1855, and when Queensland was separated from New South Wales in 1859 it got the same status immediately. Only Western Australia, so poor that for many years it needed help to support its sparse population, had to wait until 1890.

It may seem obvious to anyone looking back that Australia was all one country and should have one government, but many of the people who lived there at the time thought differently. The colonies were very independent of one another, not to say jealous. They could not even agree to build their railways to the same gauge. Political arguments were vigorous and often radical, partly because many Chartists had moved here from Britain after 1848, and trade unions were strong. There were rivalries between different groups. When some colonies decided to protect industries being founded in the cities by erecting customs barriers against foreign imports, and even against other Australian colonies, this annoyed people like the sheep-farmers who could sell their produce better under a free-trade system. Generally the colonial governments looked after the interests of the workers. As early as 1885 Victoria had boards to decide wages in some industries, and the desire to keep wages high was the main reason why the colonies began to restrict immigration. Cheap labour was not wanted. This particularly meant keeping out coloured people. At the time of the gold rush many Chinese had arrived, and later South Sea islanders had been brought as cheap – indeed, almost slave – labour on Queensland farms. This led to the beginning of a 'Keep Australia White' movement, and people realised that Australians might be stronger

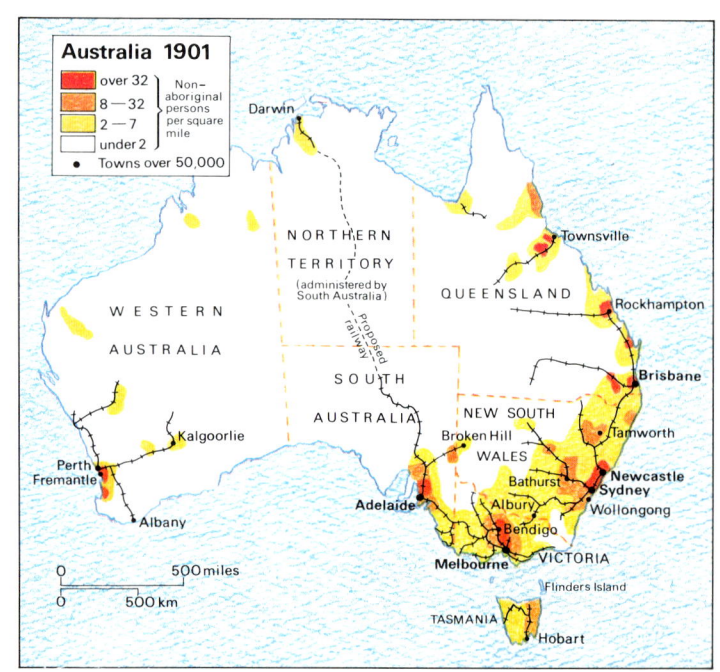

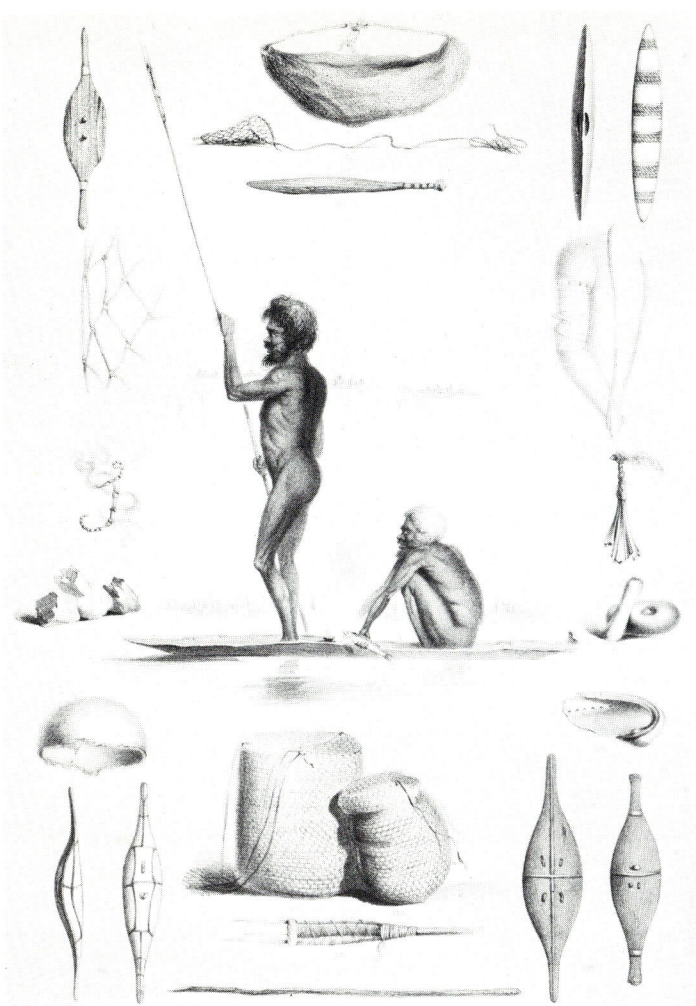

Aborigines and some of their tools, which looked primitive but were skilfully designed, made and used. The picture is from 'South Australia Illustrated', by G. F. Angas, published in 1847.

the colonies, supported by a referendum, agreed that they should join in a federation. Britain agreed, and on the first day of the twentieth century, 1 January 1901, the Commonwealth of Australia came into being.

We have traced the rise of the second great self-governing dominion of the British Empire as if it had grown in an empty land. In effect, this is the truth, for the aborigines had as little influence on the creation of the colonies and commonwealth as had the equally strange native animals. They were apparently the most primitive people that European settlers, in their expansion all over the world, had yet encountered. It was difficult for Europeans to meet these hunters and food-gatherers, whose continent since pre-history had been practically cut off from the rest of the world, as equal human beings. It was fatally easy to be blind to the complex customs and cultures of these tribes, and to see them as inferiors who must fit in with the superior ways of the white man, or move away to the least fertile lands, or die out. There was no place for their ancient skill at surviving in the wilderness, now that Australia was part of the community of civilised European states.

The most unfortunate of all were the natives of Van Diemen's Land. Cut off even from the mainland of Australia for many centuries (unlike the Pacific islanders, these people seem never to have tried to master the sea) they made do with fewer and fewer possessions and appeared utterly remote from nineteenth-century European civilisation. By the 1820s, partly as a result of the brutalities of bushrangers, the natives and the white settlers killed each other on sight. In 1835 a Nonconformist missionary managed to persuade the surviving natives to surrender, promising good treatment. But disease finished the work that the bullet had begun. The last 300 were taken to a reservation on Flinders Island. In 1844 only forty-four remained. They were taken back to Van Diemen's Land. By now they were being regarded as scientific curiosities; were they the 'missing link' between man and ape? Their skulls and skeletons were prizes for museum curators in Europe as well as Australia. In 1869 the last 'pure-blooded' Tasmanian man died, and in 1876 the last woman. Knowing what had happened to the bodies of so many of the others, she begged for a decent burial. But her bones were put on display in the local museum, and it was a hundred years before her dying wish was granted.

in their dealings with the rest of the world if they were united.

By the 1890s, too, Australians were becoming aware that the British Empire was not the only one in the world. France, Germany and the U.S.A. were competing with Britain for islands in the Pacific and their warships were uncomfortably near to Australia. After much argument, the governments of

New Zealand: the new British Isles

For nearly two centuries after Tasman discovered them, the twin islands of New Zealand seemed even less attractive to Europeans than Australia. The land seemed fertile enough, but it was even more isolated, and the natives, the Maoris, were big, intelligent people who could be formidable enemies. Nevertheless, in the early nineteenth century white men began to settle on the coasts.

The first regular visitors were British and U.S. whalers looking for water and food. Then a few traders came to supply them and to trade with the Maoris. The Maoris were quick to see the advantages of firearms, and gladly gave flax and timber in exchange for muskets and powder. The traders were a hard-bitten lot, including ex-convicts from Australia, but soon they were joined by a very different set of people. Clergymen in Australia and then in Britain heard that the Maoris seemed to be well able to understand the white men's ways, and it ought to be possible to convert them to Christianity. During the 1820s several missionaries settled in New Zealand, and sometimes succeeded in stopping disputes between Maoris and Europeans.

No European government claimed New Zealand, but this was not deterring Europeans from settling. One Belgian even tried to set up as king. In Britain a group of wealthy people followed the example of the colonising societies at work in Australia, but without waiting for recognition by the government. In 1838 the New Zealand Company sent out a strong party of colonists, buying land from Maori chiefs. This, together with rumours that France was showing signs of interest, pushed the government into action. In 1840 Britain proclaimed that New Zealand was hers, and made an agreement with about 500 Maori chiefs, protecting their lands, at the Treaty of Waitangi.

Settlers came from Britain at at astonishing rate, partly because New Zealand seemed in many ways similar to Britain and partly because the Company organised very efficiently. It had settled 6,000 colonists by the end of 1841, 15,000 by mid-1844, spreading out from Cook Strait and the centres of Wellington on the north side and Nelson on the south. There were only about 5,000 Maoris in the whole South Island, and in 1847 the British government bought them out; this cleared the ground for new groups of organised colonists, and Scottish

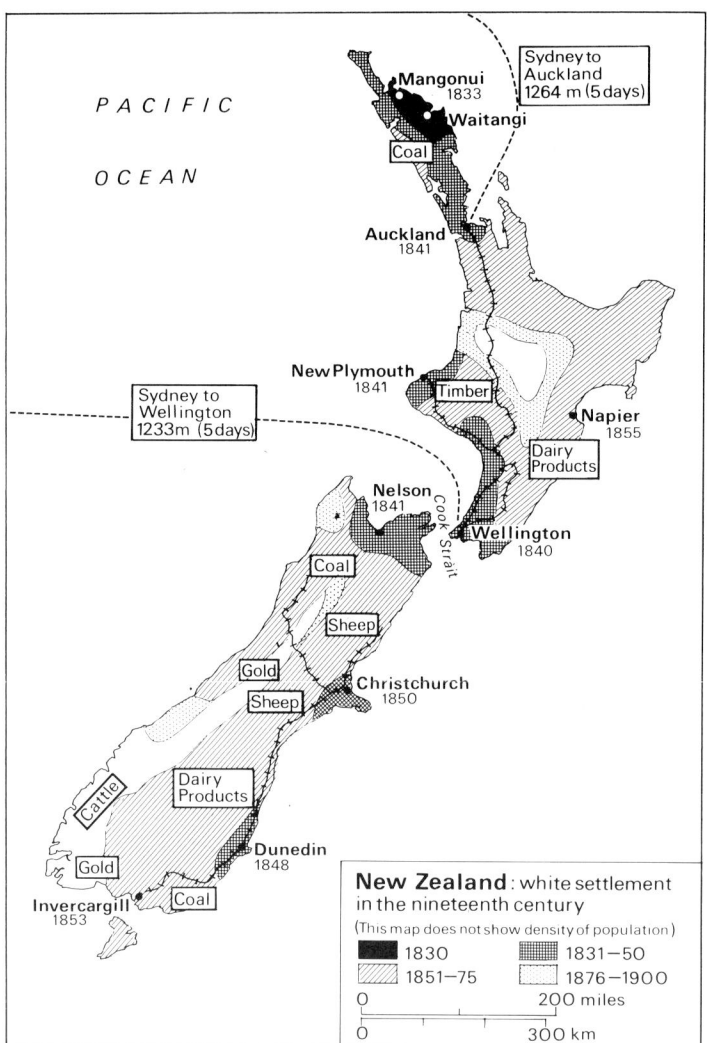

Presbyterians settled the Dunedin area in 1848, High Church Anglicans the Christchurch area in 1850. That year the New Zealand Company was dissolved, having done its work. By 1870 the white population reached 250,000, while the Maoris numbered only a fifth of that total.

Though it did well for the whites, the Company had no scruples about cheating the Maoris. It bought land from Maoris who had no right to sell it, according to their own law, and when it was pointed out to them that this was breaking the

Treaty of Waitangi they replied that the treaty was only 'a praiseworthy device for amusing and pacifying savages for the moment'. Of course this sort of behaviour led to war. The first war, 1843–6, was ended partly by the superior force of the British, partly by the governor insisting that the settlers respect the treaty. But it was difficult to ensure this, especially as the Maoris seemed to have a great amount of land that they never used and the whites' numbers were increasing. Land disputes continued, there was further fighting during the 1860s and eventually the Maoris were left with only about half the land in the North Island, and that not the best. Even so, they had done better than most 'natives' beset by European colonists in the nineteenth century.

The colonists prospered, like the Australians, mainly because of their sheep. In 1882 the New Zealand Shipping Company introduced refrigerator ships and the farmers found that mutton and lamb were even more profitable than wool. Soon a big dairy industry also grew up, and New Zealand became a foremost supplier of food to the industrial cities of far-off Britain.

Progress to self-government was very rapid. As early as 1846 the British government tried to give the colony a constitution, but had to drop the scheme in 1848 because the colonists simply were still too busy making a living to have time for politics. But in 1852 a system of representative government was successfully begun, and in 1856 New Zealand got responsible government. At first there was a federal system, but New Zealand was too small to need it and in 1876 all the power was transferred to the central government. In 1907 it officially became a dominion within the British Empire.

The new nation soon became famous for making laws for the welfare of its people. Like Australia, it kept the nation white, and it surpassed Australia in its social legislation. In 1894 compulsory arbitration was introduced for labour disputes, which led to greatly improved conditions and wages, and an eight-hour working day was fixed in 1897. The next year old age pensions began. By the beginning of the twentieth century, because of its size, climate and prosperity, New Zealand seemed to many people in Britain to be that part of the empire which most resembled the mother country, but to be in some ways a better, greener and more pleasant land.

South Africa: Boers, British and Bantus

In 1650 the Dutch East India Company founded a settlement at the Cape of Good Hope for the sole purpose of providing shelter and supplies for its ships on their passage to or from the Indies. The settlers were at first tightly controlled, but after some years a number of them began to move away from Cape Town and to live as cattle farmers on the plains inland. Sometimes they settled for a while in simple farmhouses, often they moved, or *trekked*, with their herds from pasture to pasture, living much of the time in their waggons. They were known by the Dutch word for farmers, *boers*. They were people of strong, independent character who did not submit to any authority except their Church. Even here they appointed their own pastors, but they revered the Word of God as they understood it from the Bible. They were Calvinists of the Dutch Reformed Church, and believed that it was God's will that they should, like the Chosen People of the Old Testament, possess the land and be served by the heathen. The heads of families ruled their wives and children like patriarchs, and also their coloured servants and slaves. These were mainly brown Hottentots, the most numerous native people in South Africa when the Dutch arrived.

The British government, when it took over the Cape as a result of the Napoleonic Wars, wanted it for exactly the same reason as the Dutch, and at first had no intention of interfering with the Boers. But British missionaries also arrived, and it was not long before they and the Boers were bitterly opposed. The missionaries saw South Africa as a land where they might convert the simple natives to a pure Christian way of life, if only they could save them from being debased and corrupted by other white men. They thought that the Africans should have the same rights as Europeans, that they should legally be equal. To the Boers this was not only the sort of talk that would lead to revolt and massacre; it was also directly against what God had commanded.

With their tradition that every family or small community had the right and duty under God to decide its own conduct, the Boers resented even the mildest assertion of authority from the government; now irritation and mistrust grew. Many became convinced that the British intended to break them, and that every time there was a dispute between Boer and native, the British officials would decide against the Boer. The

This picture is from another book by G. F. Angas, 'The Kaffirs Illustrated', 1849. (Kaffir was the name commonly applied to all the Bantu peoples of South Africa.) It shows something of the military equipment and organisation of the Zulus; each regiment had its own coloured pattern on its shields, the senior regiments having the most white. It also shows a Zulu kraal *or town in the background. A kraal could be of almost any size, but followed the same plan: houses neatly arranged in a circle, with the central space for drill, dancing or to keep cattle.*

final blow came in 1833 when slavery was abolished throughout the British Empire. The Boers felt humiliated in having to treat their former slaves as free men, and the compensation they received for the loss of this valuable property was, they believed, ridiculously small. Many eventually swallowed their resentment and stayed on their farms; these became known as the Cape Dutch. Others decided that British courts and British officials would go on interfering more and more, and that they would no longer stay under British rule. They must pack their waggons and take their herds and go beyond the limits of British territory. So in 1834 the Great Trek began.

While white people were spreading into South Africa from their landing-place in the south-west, a long migration of black peoples had been continuing from the north-east. These were the Bantu, virile nations that included such notable warriors as the Basuto, the Matabele and the Zulu. In the early years of the nineteenth century the Zulus came under the ferocious genius of Shaka. He invented a new method of fighting, using a short stabbing *assegai* rather than the throwing type of spear, and forming his warriors into disciplined *impis*. Their obedience was total, and there was only one punishment for failure: death. With these irresistible legions Shaka swept south-east Africa in what became known as the *mfecane*, the crushing. Tribes were driven away or killed, or sometimes amalgamated into the Zulu Empire. The empty land was filled by the cattle of the Zulus, for this was their most prized form of wealth. The Zulus made the area that the white men called Natal their special dominion, though they inhabited only part of it and the rest, where once other peoples had dwelt, was left empty. A few English traders were allowed to settle at Port Natal, because their goods and news might be useful, and one or two missionaries who visited the royal *kraal* were tolerantly received, though to his own people the Zulu king often behaved like a blood-thirsty tyrant. Shaka was murdered in 1828, but his successor Dingaan was just as cruel; a king of the Zulus could not afford to show any sign of softness.

The Boers of the Great Trek were not one organised host. They trekked in many independent waggon trains, and came together only when they wished. On the whole, though, they moved in two directions from the Cape Colony. Some went north across the rivers Orange and then Vaal. Parts of this land had been emptied by the series of wars begun by the Zulus, but much of it was claimed by the Matabele. The Boers defeated the Matabele, who retreated far to the north, so that the Boers could safely settle on widely scattered farmsteads over the vast grazing lands beyond the rivers.

The other main body was attracted by reports of the fertility of Natal. As they moved there, their leaders visited Dingaan and persuaded him to allow them to settle in the empty lands of southern Natal. But Dingaan was setting a trap. Alarmed by what he had heard of the fighting powers of the Boers who had beaten the Matabele, he intended to wait until these ones were off their guard and then massacre all of them. His plan nearly succeeded. He killed the Boer leaders when they came to ratify the treaty at his kraal, and attacked the unsuspecting waggon camps at the same time. But the Boers recovered, and soon afterwards they inflicted a heavy defeat on the impis at what became known as Blood River. Soon a new king seized power among the Zulus, with Boer help, and the Boers seemed at last to have won a safe home in Natal.

However, the British government had not decided whether it should allow the Boers to assert independence; one view was that Britain was still responsible for their behaviour, and could not shirk this duty, and another was that the Boers might cause trouble if they were allowed freedom. The government hesitated for years, but in 1842, prompted partly by the fear that other European powers might step in, proclaimed that Natal was a British colony. Two years later the Natal Boers trekked again, this time to join those who had already made their homes over the Orange and Vaal. Here they set up a number of small republics, which after much argument were formed into the Orange Free State (1854) and the South African Republic, sometimes known as the Transvaal (1856). After more hesitations, the British recognised their independence.

The situation was complicated. The two British colonies of the Cape and Natal were growing as more settlers arrived from Britain; there were the two Boer republics; and there were the blacks, who outnumbered the whites vastly. Some of them lived within the colonies or the republics, and many of these worked for the whites. But others remained independent on lands that the whites had never occupied. Borders were vague, cattle strayed – and often were stolen. Disputes easily arose, and often flared into minor wars. Gradually, as a result of these wars, the British were taking over more and more of the tribal lands. The British government did not want any more trouble and expense, but was beginning to think that the only sure way of bringing peace and justice to the land was for it all to be brought into the British Empire.

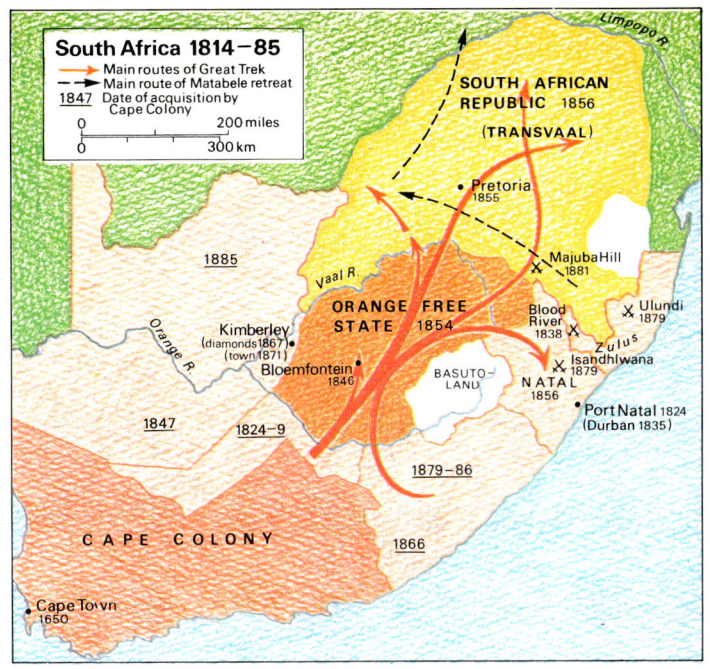

The Boers could hardly be expected to agree. They liked the British as little as ever. In 1867 diamonds were discovered in an area where the border was vague. (The town of Kimberley sprang up from the mining camps.) Britain seized it, to the disgust of the Boers. But the Boers were aware of their danger. The Zulu army, after a period of quiet, had a new king, Cetshwayo, and was retraining as if for war; and many whites feared that a Zulu attack, if combined with a rising of blacks throughout South Africa, could wipe out the whites. Must the whites stand together? British statesmen made suggestions for a federal union on the Canadian model, but few of the Boers liked the idea. Nevertheless, in 1877 the local British representative declared Transvaal part of the British Empire, and the Boer leaders, though they protested, did not resist.

The battle at Majuba Hill. This picture, by the Boer artist Otto Landsberg, gives an idea of the scene but is not wholly accurate; Paul Kruger, President of the Transvaal from 1883, is shown on horseback at the bottom left of the picture though he was not present at the battle.

Almost immediately there came the struggle with the Zulus that many people had come to see as inevitable. The British governor in South Africa seized an opportunity to force King Cetshwayo to fight. The red soldiers, as the Zulus called them, invaded Zululand in January 1879 and met disaster; one force was completely destroyed at Isandhlwana. The heroic defence of the little post at Rorke's Drift, nearby, on the same day did something to save British self-respect, though it could not replace the losses. But the Zulus failed to exploit their victory, the British recovered, and in July finally smashed the Zulu army at Ulundi. Perhaps the assegai was bound to fail in the end against the breech-loading rifle. Now that the great Bantu military power was crushed, the whites in South Africa need fear a black rising no longer.

This seemed to the Transvaal Boers to be a good time to regain their independence, especially when they heard that a new Prime Minister had come to power in Britain. It was Gladstone, who had disapproved of the annexation in 1877. But Gladstone hesitated, the Boers declared independence and the nearest British troops marched in. At Majuba Hill in February 1881 the British were defeated. Gladstone had not intended to fight and was willing to grant the Boers independence, but to do so now might look like weakness. On the other hand, a serious war to conquer the Boers might arouse the hostility of the Cape Dutch and altogether prove very expensive – and, apart from the discovery of diamonds, South Africa had been a poor country that cost the British government more than it was really worth. Eventually Gladstone decided that it was best to recognise the independence of the Transvaal.

We shall interrupt the story of South Africa at this point. We have seen how three off-shoots of Britain were established in Canada, Australia and New Zealand and grew to independence during the nineteenth century. In those three new countries the story was mainly one of peaceful progress. South Africa was proving different; there were large numbers of warlike natives and there were non-British whites who refused to become British. By the 1880s the military power of the blacks had been broken, and there was no doubt that white men ruled. But there was no real agreement between the two main groups of whites, Boers and British.

3 Opening the Orient

India: the making of the British Raj

In Asia, Europeans were not dealing with weak or primitive natives, but with civilisations that were at least as old as their own and perhaps in some ways more advanced. At first they came as traders, depending on the protection of Asian kings. It was only when trouble arose in these kingdoms and when the Europeans discovered that they must – and could – rely on their own strength that they began to dominate Eastern states. But there was never any likelihood that white men would settle in Asia as they had in the Americas, Australia and New Zealand, and parts of Africa.

British power in India began to grow when the Mogul emperors ceased to be able to keep order. The French and British East India Companies fought each other for trading advantages, and in doing this they allied themselves with Indian princes and so got involved in Indian politics. The British beat the French, and when that series of wars ceased in 1767 they had become one of the strongest powers in the Indian sub-continent, ruling some of the wealthiest parts.

From this point onwards the British Company had to go forward or back. Like any other Indian ruler, it got involved in disputes and wars with neighbours. Unlike the others, though, the British always won. So, from the late eighteenth century onwards, the Company steadily took over more regions to rule directly, or bound Indian rulers to be its allies and always to accept the advice of British envoys who came to live at their courts.

Naturally, many Indian rulers came to fear and distrust the intentions of the British. At the same time many British were coming to think that their success was the reward for their all-round superiority over the Indians. They thought that the British won because they not only had better technical devices, especially in warfare, but they also were morally and intellectually better. At first many of the British in India had respected the civilisation of the Hindus and Muslims, but as

Early nineteenth-century drawings illustrate the variety of peoples in India: a man and woman of the rice-pounder caste, Malabar, about 1828; a grain seller from Patna or Benares, about 1850; a Rajput pilot from Mandvi, Cutch, about 1835.

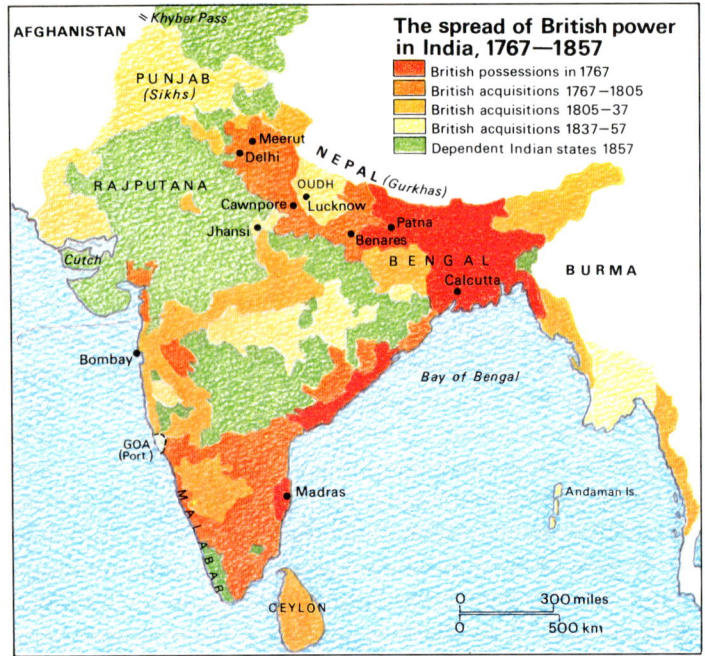

Britain became even stronger and more self-confident they seemed to see mainly the poverty, corruption and cruelty that existed in India, and to believe that these were the result of Indian ignorance and superstition. The British became convinced that they, who of course knew better – conveniently forgetting the misery in their own land – had a duty to improve India.

Trade increased, and India became more and more profitable to British manufacturers (notably Lancashire cotton-mill owners) and merchants. Meanwhile British governors of the 1830s and 1840s tried to do good to India. They forbade *suttee*, the custom of Hindu widows burning themselves to death on the funeral pyres of their husbands. They put down the *thugs*, a religious sect who thought it good to murder people, mostly travellers. Bandits were suppressed. Roads were improved. A postal service was begun, telegraph lines were set up, and a start was made on building railways. English became the official language in all parts of British India, and schools were founded to teach Indian boys the latest European knowledge. Law courts were made to work on the English pattern, with no privileges for anyone, no matter how high-born. There were attempts to make the systems of land-holding and taxation less hard on the poor. It seemed obvious to the British that all these things were for the good of India.

Many Indians, though, were unhappy. Hindus could accept that suttee and thuggee were not essential parts of their religion; indeed, some Hindus had long been strongly against what they condemned as these corruptions in their religion. But the British seemed to want to treat all groups of Indians as equal and make them mix together. To people who believed that the differences between castes had a deep spiritual meaning, that higher castes could be debased by contact with lower and that this would bring great suffering in the next life, this was a terrible danger. The confident overbearing attitude of some British made it easy to believe that they intended to undermine Indian religions and make all the people Christians, by fraud or force if necessary. This worried Muslims as well as Hindus.

The British authorities took no notice of what they thought were the ridiculous fears of a few fanatics and of ignorant peasants who must do what they were told. The governor in the early 1850s was so sure of the advantages of British rule that he began to take over states where the ruler died without leaving a son. It had been the custom for adopted heirs to succeed to thrones in India, and now the British were stepping in as over-lords and taking the kingdoms for themselves. The disinherited princes and their followers bitterly resented it, and they were not consoled by the pensions the British gave them. The British excuse for this policy of 'lapse', as it was called, was that in many Indian states the people were badly ruled, subject to grinding taxes and inhuman punishments. This may have been true, but it was not necessarily the badly ruled states that lapsed, and in some cases British rule was no improvement. To many people it looked simply like greed and ambition. It was all very disturbing and confusing.

But who exactly *were* the British who were doing these things? This too was confusing. Officially, the East India Company still ruled. In fact, the Company had long ceased to be a trading organisation; it was now entirely occupied with administering its territories, and the British government had control over the men who managed the Company in London. So who was really in charge? Ultimately it was the British government, but only in an indirect, slow, complicated way.

Similarly, the army was under two systems. Most of the troops belonged to the Company's army, but there were also several regiments from the regular British army, known as the King's (after 1837, Queen's) troops.

In the last resort, British power rested on the army. Most of the soldiers were Company's troops, and most of these were sepoys, Indians armed and trained in the European style. The sepoy regiments had a long record of brave and faithful service. Their British officers trusted them and were proud of them, though new officers were coming who, it was grumbled, did not know the men as the old ones did. Some experienced and perceptive officers complained that the government was behaving so foolishly that it was undermining the sepoys' loyalty. Hindu soldiers had been ordered overseas, contrary to what they had been promised, and punished when they refused. Extra payments for distant service had been withdrawn. Many soldiers came from Oudh, a kingdom which was seized by the government in 1856; so they feared that this would deprive them of a special status they had enjoyed as men from an independent state, and were angry at what they

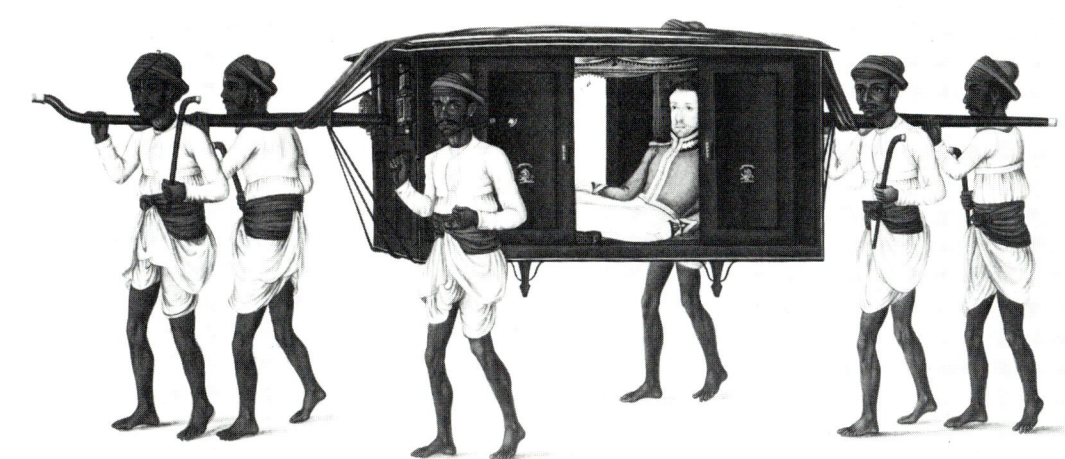

A representative of the latest ruling race to come to India: a British officer in his litter, about 1828.

The Diwan (chief minister) of Delhi Babu Ram, and his adopted son, about 1825.

A sweet-meat seller from Patna or Benares, about 1850.

British troops – Highlanders with white 'Havelock' covers on their caps to keep off the sun – encamped beside a tree loaded with hanged rebels. An illustration from C. Bell's 'History of the Mutiny in India', published in 1859. A British officer reported that he had heard of 127 rebels hanged on one tree, and added: 'These dreadful, though absolutely necessary severities are most painful to recollect and to commemorate.' His attitude does not seem to have been typical.

took to be an insult to their old rulers. The Company's army was in three parts: Bengal, Madras and Bombay. Of these, the Bengal army was the biggest, and it also had most grievances. But the authorities did not see the danger.

Mutiny was sparked off in the Bengal army by the new greased-paper cartridge. The grease was meant to keep the powder dry, but soldiers got some on their lips and teeth when they bit the cartridges open to load their rifles. A rumour went round among the sepoys that the grease contained the fat of cows and pigs. To the Hindu, the cow is sacred; to the Muslim, the pig is unclean. Men of both religions would be defiled. Many sepoys refused to use the new cartridge and were dismissed or punished. Then on 10 May 1857 the sepoy regiments stationed at Meerut rose, killed several Europeans, and marched to take the old capital, Delhi.

The mutiny became a revolt that spread across northern India. It was unorganised, confused, bursting out in many places where different people had different reasons for wanting to get rid of the British. Other Indians remained loyal and fought for the British. Southern India and the Bombay and Madras troops did not rise. British writers usually call it the Indian Mutiny; but, though it began as a mutiny, it became something much bigger. Indian writers often call it the Great Rebellion, suggesting that it was a rising of the Indian peoples as a whole; this is also wrong, because most Indians were either neutral or pro-British. It was so chaotic that no label can be accurate.

It was also very bloody. In some places the rebels massacred the British, including women and children; Cawnpore was where the most notorious slaughter took place. The government forces replied by killing every rebel or suspected rebel. Each side also had its heroes, like the British who held the Residency at Lucknow or, on the rebel side, the dispossessed Rani of Jhansi who died sword in hand at the head of her troops. At the time, though, it was the cruelty rather than the heroism which seemed important. *Punch* expressed the British demand for vengeance:

'Who pules about mercy? The agonised wail
 Of babies hewn piecemeal still sickens the air
 And echoes still shudder that caught on the gale
 The mother's – the maiden's wild scream of despair.

'Who pules about mercy? That word may be said
 When steel, red and sated, perforce must retire,
 And, for every soft hair of each dearly-loved head,
 A cord has despatched a foul fiend to hell-fire.'

It was only after the revolt had been stamped out in a year of merciless battle and punishment that it became possible to try to learn the lessons.

The first thing to do was to end the old confusion about who was responsible for governing British India. On 1 November 1858 a royal proclamation declared that henceforth the Crown – which meant the British government – took direct control. The Company was ended. On 1 January 1877 the government took the final step of proclaiming Queen Victoria Empress of India, the most exalted title possible. India was now classed as one united empire in its own right, with the imperial viceroy reigning over all. As far as titles went, the British *Raj* (rule) could not be greater. What did it achieve in practice?

THE ARMY was reorganised completely. More troops were recruited from those peoples who, like the Sikhs and Gurkhas, had proved their loyalty in the dark days of 1857, fewer from other parts. British troops were always placed in the most strategic positions. The new army was well treated, and soon became a proud and very trustworthy force. There was little danger of the sort of bad feeling that made the Mutiny possible.

THE PRINCES were treated with respect. No more 'lapse' took place, there were no more attempts to seize their states. Even if a prince were to be accused of ruling his people unjustly, the viceroy would not take any action against him without the advice of the other princes. There were to be no more cases like those of Oudh or Jhansi.

ADMINISTRATION was reorganised, so that the Indian Civil Service became a very attractive career to ambitious young men from Britain. The entrance examinations were hard, and so was the work expected of the men appointed. But they were given posts of great power over the districts to which they were appointed, and earned a reputation for intelligence, honesty and for looking after their people. The most important posts, especially at first, were reserved for British, but a vast number of jobs in the government service were open to Indians.

EDUCATION was needed by Indians in such posts, whether they were humble clerks or dignified lawyers and judges, and there was a great expansion of schools and colleges to give European learning to boys aiming at such careers.

Part of a Sikh regiment on parade, about 1880, proud and trusted soldiers who despised those who had betrayed their salt.

COMMUNICATIONS were developed, especially a railway system which soon cast a steel net across the whole subcontinent. The railways held India together as nothing in the past had ever done. Of course the viceroy could use them to move soldiers about if there were any trouble, but mostly they allowed Indians to travel and trade and get to know their own great land.

All this gave the government a firm grip on India, and from a European point of view it was a great step forward because a more efficient government would be better for the country. In fact, did it make much difference to the people? Many got good jobs serving the Raj as lawyers and officials, as clerks, perhaps, or railwaymen. Factories began to be built in the expanding cities and another new Western-educated class appeared, the industrialists and businessmen. But these were only a tiny minority. The overwhelming majority of Indians, whatever their nation or religion, were peasants who lived at the mercy of the climate. When the crops failed, they died.

The government tried to help by irrigation schemes which brought water from the hills in dry seasons. Nothing could really replace the monsoon, though, and when it failed there were still terrible droughts. In the famine of 1876–8 about five million starved to death, even though the government spent

£11m bringing in food. But the system did improve. In 1899–1900 one million people died, but it was estimated that government relief saved 6 million.

In other ways, too, the viceroy's government tried to make the hard lives of most Indians a little less hard. The terms on which peasants rented their lands were made to favour the landlords less. As industries began to grow in the towns, factory laws were passed to give the workers some protection. Above all, there was a steady effort to improve cleanliness in villages and towns, and to reduce the death-rate from disease.

But the land and its populations and their problems were enormous, and some people felt that any improvements were only scratching the surface; in the end, it would always be Nature that dictated the conditions of life in India. Still the British were determined to hold on to the Indian Empire. Why?

Many British officials undoubtedly thought that they were doing something that was a worthwhile, even a noble duty, and many enjoyed the power and privileges that went with being a *sahib*. But Britain's link with India was by now a feeling that arose from a long tradition. The quest for oriental wealth had been behind the fifteenth- and sixteenth-century voyages of discovery and had led, sometimes indirectly, to the foundation of most European colonies. India itself was still the source of great trade, and also the base from which British interests could spread further – to Ceylon, Burma, Malaya and into the China Seas. But wealth was not all. Ruling India was different, more grand and imperial than colonising virgin plains and forests. Holding India gave some British a sense that they were a great imperial people, like the Romans. And they had to guard the Indian Empire against the age-old threat of invasion from the north-west. Through the passes in those mountains, passes like the Khyber, every invasion of India had come, until the Europeans had arrived by sea. Now the British–Indian army guarded the plains and cities against attack from the warrior tribes of the Afghan frontier. Behind the tribesmen some British suspected a far greater threat, the Russian Empire that was spreading through Central Asia. To many British, India was altogether a fascinating place, exotic, challenging and full of adventure and rich rewards.

left: The terminus of the Indian Peninsular Railway at Bombay, built in 1866, is a huge pile of Victorian Gothic which could be seen as a symbol of the way the British were imposing their own ideas.

right: A station-master and engine-driver at Vellore, about 1880. Like many of the men who operated the railways, they are Eurasians, the children of Indian mothers and British fathers. People like this, despite their valuable work, were treated as outsiders by both the British and the Indians. They were some of the most unfortunate victims of the gulf between the two cultures.

below right: A British Resident supervising famine relief, 1897.

The British felt sure that they were ruling India for the best. Indians could not rule themselves, because there were so many divisions between them that they were bound to fight unless outsiders restrained them. So Indians could be allowed to help in ruling the sub-continent, but only under British orders. There was to be no quick development of responsible government as in Canada or Australia, only a small beginning by allowing Indians to elect local councils and to raise the local rates and taxes, which met a great deal of the cost of governing India.

This was not enough for the growing number of Indians who were learning European ideas. They read of liberalism and nationalism, of parliaments and constitutions. If this was good for Europeans, they asked, why not for Indians too? In 1885 a group of them met together to form a political party. They called themselves the Indian National Congress, and pledged themselves to work peacefully towards the time when Indians alone would rule the united sub-continent of India. But though they believed in unity, they were mainly Hindus, and the Muslims felt that they were being pushed aside. They founded their own political party, the Muslim League, in 1906. Western-style party politics were taking root in India.

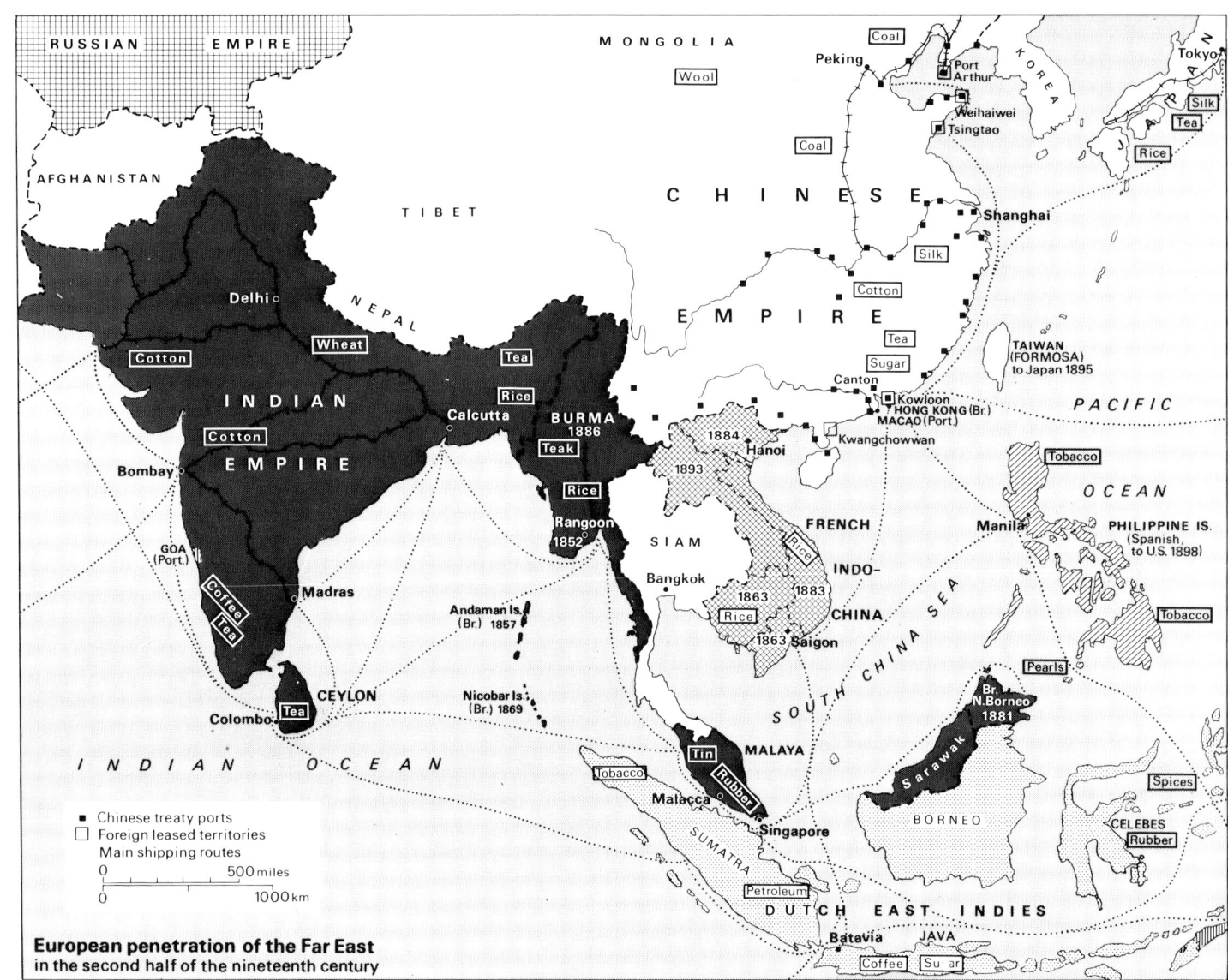

European penetration of the Far East in the second half of the nineteenth century

This map shows the overall situation across a large area, and cannot explain all the details. For example, many Indian states still had their own princes to rule them, but the princes had British advisers and were inside the Empire; while Sarawak in Borneo was not in the British Empire, but the rajah was British. Dates are given only for territory annexed in the later part of the nineteenth century, not for territory already under European control in 1850. The products named are those which were most valuable to European merchants; some, like rubber, were only becoming important at the end of the period. The map shows European power and influence spreading from the west. It is not large enough to show two other directions from which the white man came: Americans from the east, and Russians from the north.

China: the collapse of a civilisation

China was far larger than India, and had been united as one empire for two thousand years. The Chinese called their land the Middle Kingdom, and thought it the centre of the world in all respects. Outside, they thought, were lands inhabited only by people of inferior culture, at best semi-civilised and often utterly barbarous. These uncouth races had nothing to teach or to offer the Chinese. Their civilisation had remained substantially the same during the whole history of their empire, based on the precepts of Confucius and other ancient sages, and on respect for old traditions and for their ancestors. The mandarins, the officials who governed China, could qualify for their positions only through long examinations on Chinese classical literature; many students tried, but relatively few passed. Emperors came and went, but the mandarins seemed to go on for ever, learned, cultured, very sure of the superiority of their own civilisation.

It would be wrong to assume that nothing ever changed in China. There were times of trouble, of flood or famine, rebellion, invasion and conquest by the barbarians from the steppes of central Asia beyond the Great Wall. Dynasties rose and fell. According to the Chinese, it was by the will of Heaven that an emperor reigned, and therefore he must be obeyed. But when things went badly wrong, this was a sign that Heaven was no longer pleased with the regime. So when a dynasty of emperors was overthrown and replaced by rebels or invaders, it simply meant that the new rulers now enjoyed the mandate of Heaven, because they were worthy and the old ones were not. This was a very practical doctrine. It meant that emperors could normally command complete loyalty, but that if they were very poor rulers their subjects were justified in transferring their allegiance to someone else.

Through all the rebellions and invasions the Chinese way of life went on. They had a marvellous capacity for absorbing their new masters into the old system. The last great upheaval had been the conquest by Manchus, war-like people from the north, who had put an end to the Ming dynasty of emperors in 1644. The Manchus tried to keep themselves apart, a dominant race of warriors living in China. They made the Chinese wear pigtails, while they did not. Nor did they follow the Chinese custom of binding the feet of upper-class girls so that when they grew up they could only totter feebly on these 'lily-feet'. (This was thought to be graceful, and wealthy women did not need to walk far.) But the mandarins went on running the Middle Kingdom in the traditional way. The Manchu or Ch'ing dynasty was at its height in the Ch'ien Lung reign, 1736–95. Scholarship and the arts flourished, and Chinese armies forced Burma, Nepal, Tibet and large parts of Central Asia to promise obedience to Peking. But a decline followed swiftly, even before the emperor's death. The glories had to be paid for by heavy taxes. There was discontent, then revolts. Officials, even the highest, accepted bribes. By the beginning of the nineteenth century (in the European way of measuring time) there were many signs of decay. Was this dynasty, like others in the past, going to lose the mandate of Heaven?

It was at this time that Europeans began to push for more trade with China. The Portuguese had been allowed one trading town, Macao, since the sixteenth century, and as far as the Chinese government was concerned it was quite enough for the very small amount of contact that was thought useful with the big-nosed, red-faced, hairy barbarians from the sea. In the seventeenth century Russians, through Siberia, had reached China and tried to make treaties, but they were so few and weak that they had been forced to agree to whatever terms the Chinese wanted. It was true that a handful of Jesuit missionaries had been allowed to live in Peking, where they had won the respect of Chinese scholars for their learning and intelligence; but these men dressed and lived like Chinese, and did not win converts to their Church – they were content merely to begin slowly to build understanding between Chinese and European cultures. Their approach had been too slow to please the Pope, and eventually their mission was withdrawn.

Now envoys of a new sort came to Peking. Britain, the foremost trading power, naturally took the lead. In 1796 Lord Macartney was permitted to visit the imperial court, and at once the different attitudes of East and West caused difficulty. Macartney, as representative of another sovereign, refused to kow-tow to the emperor, for he thought this a degrading gesture of inferiority. The Chinese authorities explained his refusal as being merely the ignorance of a primitive tribesman from the most remote regions of the world, and insisted on regarding him as being merely a bearer of tribute from a distant vassal. The Chinese government refused to extend

A high official performs the kow-tow, *ceremonial prostration, before the emperor while other officials attend. Their rank is displayed by the buttons and feathers in their hats, and their pig-tails show them to be Chinese, not Manchu.*

trade to more than a few merchants at Canton, and when another British envoy came in 1816 the emperor refused to see him.

Chinese aloofness did not worry some thrusting Westerners. More traders came to Canton, mainly British, and some missionaries ventured into China. They had no permission, but the Chinese were tolerant and polite people and did not interfere with them. It was the growth of trade that caused serious trouble. Canton was a long way from Peking, and at first some local officials could be persuaded to 'not notice' the illegal increase in trade. So it grew until the Chinese government became seriously worried. Opium-smoking had recently increased alarmingly in China; one possible explanation is that more and more people found life so tedious that only drugs gave them any pleasure – a sign of a doomed civilisation. The best opium was imported by British merchants from India, and they demanded silver as payment. The Chinese government was worried both by the increase in drug-taking and the loss of silver, which upset the monetary system. The merchants took no notice. They went on with their profitable trade; if people wanted to buy, why should they not earn an honest living by selling?

This situation flared into violence. In 1839 Chinese officials at Canton confiscated and destroyed a big quantity of opium belonging to British merchants. The British demanded compensation, the nearest British warships arrived to add force to the demand, and fighting started. This became known as the First Opium War, and there were many people in Britain who were ashamed of appearing to be fighting to force dangerous drugs on the Chinese. But the real importance of the war was that a Western power was prepared to use force to compel China to open her ports wider (opium just happened to be the commodity which brought the conflict to a head) and that it proved strong enough to do so. The small British forces defeated all the ships and soldiers that the Chinese could send against them, and they did so with astonishing ease. It revealed to the rest of the world that China, huge though she was, lacked the strength to resist modern European arms. The giant

Every year the empress and her ladies would pluck the first mulberry leaves to feed the silkworms. The painting shows the ceremony taking place at the Temple of Silkmaking, in the Sea Palaces. These palaces were nowhere near the sea but stood among lakes near Peking, where earth, water and buildings had been carefully landscaped to provide beautiful views in every direction.

was helpless. By the Treaty of Nanking in 1842 Britain was leased the island of Hong Kong as her own trading base, and was allowed to trade in the so-called treaty ports of Canton, Amoy, Foochow, Ningpo and Shanghai. What one Western power got, the others demanded also – and got. Then U.S. pressure got foreigners living in China the right to be tried by their own consuls if they were accused of offences, not by Chinese courts. French pressure made the Chinese government admit Catholic missionaries, and then it had to give the same concession to Protestants. China could not resist.

The men who governed China were badly upset, but they had little idea of what was really happening. Their ignorance of the outside world was astonishing. According to a Chinese gazetteer of the time, England was another name for Holland, and America was a small island off its coast; an official in 1850 who borrowed a foreign atlas and produced an accurate account of world geography was reprimanded for being too friendly with foreigners. After so many centuries it was impossible for the mandarins suddenly to understand that the despised barbarians had passed them by, and were far ahead in

One small paddle-steamer, HMS 'Nemesis', was strong enough to destroy a whole squadron of war-junks. It happened on 7 January 1841.

The Summer Palace outside Peking was occupied and looted by French and British troops in 1860. Soon after, it was burnt down by the British soldiers on the orders of Lord Elgin.

many fields of knowledge. Anyway, China had dealt with powerful barbarians in the past; good diplomats knew how to give way before enemies and lead them into quarrelling among themselves.

Meanwhile there were more urgent problems. Revolts were breaking out among discontented people in many parts of the empire, and one grew to an enormous size. This was the Taiping rebellion, led by a man who had put together a new religion from parts of others, including Christianity that he had heard about from missionaries. From 1850 the rebels swept over and held large parts of central and southern China, and at one time threatened Peking itself. Government troops, some of them trained or led by Europeans, managed to suppress the rebellion at last, but not until 1864, after it had cost about 30 million lives.

At the same time there was more trouble with foreigners. Further disputes about trade led to another war with Britain, this time helped by France. In 1860 the European soldiers marched into Peking. During this advance the Chinese seized some European negotiators and their escort, and treated them so badly that twenty died. The European commanders were furious at what they regarded as official Chinese treachery and cruelty, and looked for some way of punishing the people responsible – the emperor and his court, not the ordinary Chinese. They decided to destroy something that the emperor really valued. Outside Peking was a great park with a wonderful series of gardens and palaces, full of priceless works of art. It was known as the Summer Palace. The Europeans completely laid it waste. To Lord Elgin, who ordered the destruction, this was the only way of teaching a lesson to a wicked ruler who had fled, leaving his people to pay for his crimes. But to the Chinese it seemed further proof that the Western foreigners were indeed barbarians.

As if all this were not enough, more foreigners were coming, this time from the north. The Russians were renewing their eastward ambitions through Siberia, and wanted to control the River Amur and find a good harbour near its mouth which would be the base for merchant ships, and possibly some warships, working in the China Seas and the Pacific. They took the opportunity to make their requests when the Chinese government, facing Taipings, British and French, was not going to involve itself in more trouble over a remote stretch of frontier territory. Russia got what she wanted and set about building Vladivostok in 1860.

far left: *Kuo Sung-t'ao, 1818–91, first Chinese ambassador to the West. He himself respected Westerners, but this made powerful people in the Chinese government distrust him and his career did not prosper.*

left: *Tzu Hsi, 1835–1908, the Dowager Empress. The long fingernails with their exquisitely decorated covers showed that she performed no manual work, but they did not prevent her from being an accomplished writer with brush and ink, an art greatly respected and admired in China.*

At last the government began to show signs of taking the foreign threat seriously. In 1861 a Foreign Ministry was founded, something that had never been thought necessary when all foreigners were treated as mere savages. In 1863 British officials were appointed to organise a new customs service, which not only proved efficient, honest and profitable, but also did a great deal to improve the harbours and navigational aids around the coasts of China. A navy board was set up and began to buy modern warships. The army was partly reorganised and armed with modern weapons. The first railway was opened in 1888, and soon coal-mining and steelmaking became growing Chinese industries. In the 1870s Chinese students began to be sent to Europe and America to learn modern technologies, and in 1875 the first Chinese resident ambassador to a foreign government took up his post in London.

But these beginnings were small in comparison with the size of China, and many leading Chinese resented them bitterly because they implied that China was recognising foreigners as equals. One high official at the Foreign Ministry said that nobody with any sense of honour could actually *study* foreign affairs, and many officials tried to resign rather than accept appointments in the Foreign Ministry. A few mandarins were prepared to admit that foreigners really did deserve respect. More would admit that the Western barbarians had discovered a few technical tricks which made them stronger than the Chinese, but argued that this was sheer accident and had nothing to do with the basic superiority of Chinese ways. The Chinese must tolerate the barbarians only up to the point where they learned their technical tricks, and then they could once more assert their true position. Many mandarins were reluctant even to admit this.

With the ruling class divided thus, the decision of the emperor himself was especially important. But there was no effective emperor. In 1861 an emperor died young, and there had to be a regency for his infant successor. This soon became dominated by the Dowager Empress Tzu Hsi, and by fair means and foul she managed to retain power until her death in 1908, with only brief intervals, for she brought up one young emperor after another to do as she willed. The princes were unhealthy and died young – it truly seemed that the Ch'ing dynasty was losing the mandate of Heaven. Tzu Hsi lacked enough authority to force major reforms on her very reluctant empire, and anyway she did not want to. She usually took the side of anti-foreign ministers and officials. Sometimes this meant that even the reforms that had been made became useless; for example, in 1890 she dissolved the Navy Board, which had been doing well, so that the navy quickly fell into

The breakdown of imperial China, 1840–1900

neglect while her favourites pocketed the money that should have gone to the sailors.

So the rot went on. China had to recognise the loss of her outer fringe of tributary states: Burma to Britain, the Indo-China provinces to France, Korea as an independent kingdom strongly influenced by Japan. Sometimes the foreigners used force to back their demands, and the most shocking disaster came in 1894 when, in a war over Korea, Japan destroyed the Chinese army and navy. This was the signal for all the other foreign powers – there were more now, including Germany and Italy – to demand even greater trading privileges, more treaty ports and areas known as 'spheres of influence' within China itself. At the same time more and more missionaries were penetrating all parts of the empire, trying to turn people away from their old ideas to believe in foreign gods.

Chinese reacted in two opposite ways. Some demanded sweeping reforms; to bring the country up to the level of the Westerners China must sincerely adopt a great amount of

Western thinking. Others believed that the only hope was to rise against all forms of Western influence and force the foreigners out, and that China could do it if she were properly roused. In 1898 the young emperor decided that the reform arguments were right, and he issued a flood of reform proclamations about education, finance, transport, the army and the navy. Everything was to be changed, old habits and privileges were to be swept away. But he was a young man who had been brought up with no experience of politics (Tzu Hsi had seen to that) and the reformers he trusted were fanatics with equally little idea of how to get things done. The episode is known as the Hundred Days of Reform, because at the end of that time the Dowager Empress regained power. The emperor's rashness had alarmed the leaders of the army, and they arrested and imprisoned him on Tzu Hsi's orders.

Next it was the turn of the violent traditionalists. There was a widespread movement for the purpose of encouraging physical training, partly encouraged by officials in order to form a kind of militia. The Chinese name for the movement was Harmonious Fists, and in English the members were usually called the Boxers. They hated the way foreigners were destroying China, and their rage burst out against foreign missionaries and Chinese who had become Christians. In many parts of China there were riots, and missionaries and their converts were killed, sometimes cruelly. The foreign ambassadors in Peking protested, but many high officials were secret supporters of the Boxers, and so was the Dowager Empress herself. Thousands of Boxers surged into Peking in the summer of 1900, and attacked the foreign legations which were defended only by a few hundred embassy guards. The Dowager Empress told the defenders to surrender, and when they refused she ordered the imperial army to join in the attack. But once again it was the generals who really decided the outcome. Though they dared not disobey openly, they knew that if the Europeans were massacred – which would certainly happen if the Boxers overran the legations – the European powers would combine to take such a revenge that China would be smashed to pieces. So the defenders were able to hold out until an international relief column reached the city after two months. The Boxer movement collapsed. It was the end of the attempt to expel the Europeans by force.

It seemed now that the Middle Kingdom had no hope of survival.

The main tower of Himeji Castle, built by the son-in-law of the first Tokugawa shogun *between 1601 and 1609. Though highly decorated, the castle was exceedingly strong, with three smaller central towers to support this one, fortified connecting passages, complex walled compounds and moats.*

Japan: a nation transformed

During the anxious days of the siege at Peking the Japanese soldiers were the heroes whom everybody liked. The different European groups often grumbled and complained about one another, but never about the Japanese. Those brave, cheerful little soldiers always did their duty magnificently and they never complained. Fifty years before, the Japanese had been even more cut off from the ways of Westerners than the Chinese had been, yet now they were taking their stand beside the European nations and earning their admiration. Japan had resolutely done everything that China had failed to do, and was reaping the reward.

In the early seventeenth century the Japanese government had become alarmed by the behaviour of European traders and missionaries, had expelled all foreigners and forbidden Japanese to travel abroad. The islands were cut off from the outside world except that Dutch merchants were allowed, under strict regulations, to have a trading post on Deshima Island in Nagasaki Bay. Then the rulers of Japan tried to maintain their land true to what they believed to be its fine old traditions.

There was an emperor but, unlike the Chinese emperor, he was merely a ceremonial figure, living powerless in the ancient

This contemporary Japanese print represents the scene when Perry anchored off the coast. It gives a lively idea of how curious the Japanese were about the strangers, and what they meant when they called the U.S. vessels 'the black ships'.

capital, Kyoto. For centuries the power had rested in the hands of a military leader called the *shogun*, and from about 1600 this office had always been occupied by members of the Tokugawa family. They contrived, sometimes by force but usually by making agreements, to rule with the help of the great lords, or *daimyo*, who dominated the provinces. The shogun himself ruled from Edo. All these men belonged to a warrior class called the *samurai*, and so did the many thousands who served them as soldiers and, increasingly, as stewards and administrators. The samurai were supposed to live according to a strict code of military honour called *bushido*, the way of the warrior. They ruled the land, demanding the respect of the lower ranks – peasants, craftsmen and merchants. The mandarins who were the ruling class in China were men of letters who tended to despise violence. The ruling class in Japan, though, were men who made a cult of the sword.

Though Japan in some ways appeared to be fixed in an unchanging culture, there was a good deal of change and growth during the centuries of isolation. Merchants were despised by the samurai, who thought it disgraceful to amass riches by selling things for more than they were worth. But the merchants prospered, and many a samurai was deeply in debt to merchants. Old Japan was a land of castles and villages and temples, but it also included great bustling cities like Osaka, full of shops and workshops and taverns and theatres, a place dedicated to the making and spending of money. Even the countryside felt such influences. Payments were reckoned in quantities of the standard crop, rice; but in fact they were always now made in money. Peasants drifted from their farms towards the cities, and among those who remained there were, by the later eighteenth century, frequent revolts which often won better conditions for them from their lords. By this time, too, there were some Japanese scholars who, reading books imported by the Dutch at Deshima, understood that knowledge was increasing among the Europeans and argued that it was time for Japan to open its gates and admit new ideas. But such voices were ignored or suppressed by the government.

The gate was forced open by the U.S.A. In 1853 Commodore M. C. Perry brought four warships to anchor in Edo Bay,

The rise of modern Japan, 1853–1910

and delivered a letter from his President asking for agreements to trade and to supply U.S. ships with food and water. He promised to return next year for a reply. The Japanese had looked carefully at his ships and guns, and were impressed. The shogun and his advisers, very unwillingly, decided that they had to agree. Of course, as soon as the U.S.A. was allowed to trade, other Western nations demanded and had to be given the same rights. European merchants and their consuls began to be seen in Japanese ports.

Many Japanese were furious, especially the proud samurai. Some of them attacked foreigners, killing and wounding a few. But this only made matters worse, as the shogun's government then had to pay compensation and give more trading concessions to the foreigners. It was a time of confusion. The south-western provinces became the centre of anti-foreign feeling, perhaps because they saw most of the foreigners. Young samurai from there were disgusted with what they considered the weakness of the shogun. They went to Kyoto to try to influence the emperor to come out of a seclusion that had lasted for many centuries, rally Japan and chastise the intruders. But when Japanese coastal guns on the south-west coast opened fire on foreign ships, a combined foreign naval force appeared and delivered such a bombardment that even those warlike patriots had to pause and think.

The situation changed in 1867 when both the shogun and the emperor died within three months. The new emperor was a young man prepared to listen to the south-westerners. The new shogun could see no way of solving Japan's problems and was unwilling to oppose the emperor. He resigned. The emperor did not appoint another shogun, but announced that he would rule himself. In 1868 he adopted a new name for his reign, *Meiji*, which has become the name for the revolution that was about to take place, and he moved the imperial court to Edo, which was now called 'the eastern capital' or Tokyo.

The ambitious young samurai who directed the government in the name of the emperor were determined to wield real power, but they quickly realised that to resist the foreigners was hopeless. Their government had to learn from those foreigners how to be powerful in nineteenth-century terms; the knights must hang up their armour and adjust their ideas to new ways of wielding power.

During the first few years of the Meiji period they changed the whole system of governing Japan. The daimyo were first reduced from being lords of their provinces to being simply governors representing the emperor; then, in 1871, they lost even this. Japan was divided into prefectures on the French model, with prefects taking orders from the emperor's ministers. The army and the navy were reorganised copying the most successful European models, the British navy and the

47

German army. In 1872 conscription was begun, so that now all Japanese were warriors, not only the samurai. It was necessary for these people to have some education and in 1871 a ministry of education was founded to ensure schooling for all Japanese. About the same time the first newspapers appeared, Japan adopted the European (Gregorian) calendar, and allowed freedom of worship to all religions.

The government knew that Japan needed economic strength too, and did its best to encourage trade and industry in the Western style. The first railway, between Tokyo and the port of Yokohama, was opened in 1872, and by the end of the century Japan had over 4,000 miles of railway. At first Japan bought the engines and machines for her factories (mainly paper and cotton mills) but by 1900 she was beginning to be able to make for herself whatever she needed, including heavy steel goods. All this was supported by a banking service copied from the U.S.A.

The achievement was enormous and rapid, but the price was high. Though the members of the government were themselves samurai, they abolished samurai privileges; the pensions that they had been allowed were stopped, and they lost their ancient right to go about wearing two swords. It seemed that the old order was to be destroyed entirely, and in 1877 a samurai revolt broke out in the south-west, led by a man who had until recently been one of the government but who thought that change had gone too far. In fierce fighting the revolt was crushed by the government's new army, the common conscripts with their European weapons and training. But the changes were not all gain for the common people; many of them suffered those same evils of working long hours for little pay in unhealthy factories that had happened to many European workers when their countries went through an industrial revolution. And many of the growing towns were foul, ugly places. Educated Japanese, including the samurai, had always cultivated a sensitive appreciation of the beauties of flowers and scenery, and now it seemed that they were having to sacrifice this too.

Amid all these changes the emperor – or, rather, the men around him – remained firmly in power. Some Japanese argued that the country should copy the Westerners in having a constitution with some sort of parliament. In 1889 a new constitution did indeed provide for an elected lower house, and a house of peers; but they had little power, and the emperor's decrees continued to have full force.

By the 1890s the Meiji revolution had already given Japan many of the qualities of a European state. Also, the population was increasing fast. The government thought that the

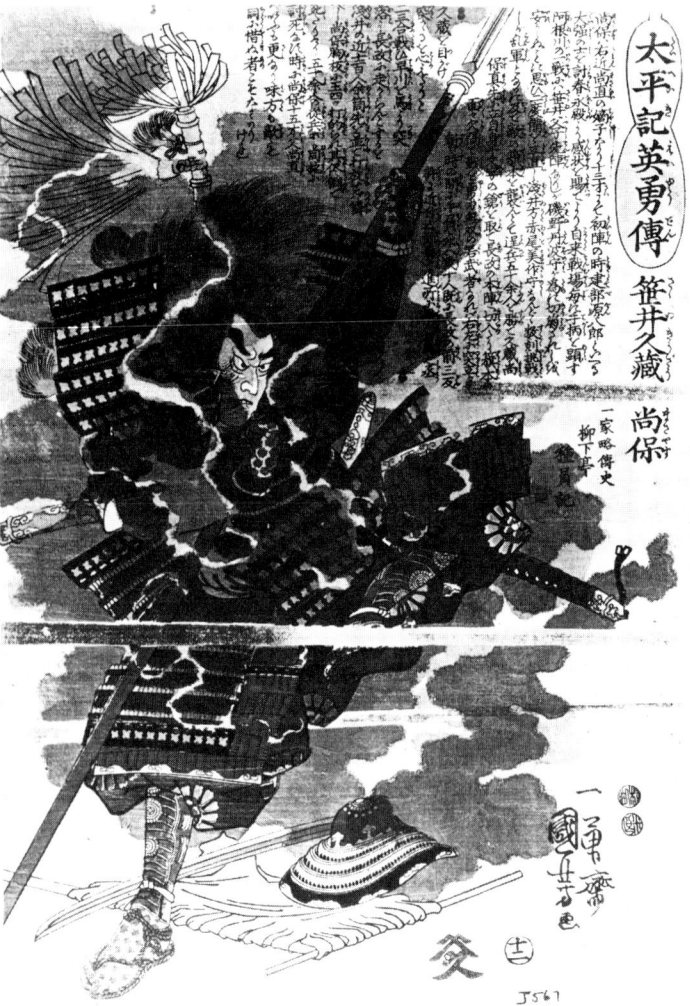

These prints sum up the apparent transformation of Japan. The old heroic fighting spirit is glorified by the artist Utabawa Kuniyoshi, 1798–1861, in his picture of a spearman in traditional samurai armour advancing into a hail of musketry. Opposite is a print of 1875, showing the opening of the new Post Office at Yokohama.

time had come for Japan to follow the European example in one more direction; imperial expansion. Korea was the obvious target. Though dependent on the Chinese Empire, Korea had its own government and royal family, and if it were declared independent the way would be clear for Japan to take it over. After a lot of wrangling and confusion over many years, this was the main cause of the war between China and Japan in 1894. As we saw, it was a sweeping victory for Japan's forces, and in the peace treaty of 1895 Japan gained the island of Formosa (Taiwan), the Pescadores, and the recognition of Korea as an independent state.

It was this last that brought Japan face to face with a dangerous rival. While most of the powers that were pulling China apart came from the south, across the sea, one was moving overland from the north: Russia. By the end of the century Russia held Port Arthur as a strongly fortified naval base in ice-free waters, and effectively controlled Manchuria, the part of the Chinese Empire that lay between Port Arthur and eastern Siberia. Port Arthur was the place where Russian

A cartoon published in a French newspaper contrasts the fortunes of China and Japan. The nations rejoicing at China's collapse are all Western except one: Italy, Britain, Japan, Russia, Germany, France and the U.S.A. The title was: 'One more good push and the colossus will be in pieces.'

Two Japanese prints glorifying their new successes in war. The first shows Chinese envoys, in their traditional costume, suing for peace from the Japanese, arrogant in their Western uniforms, at the end of the war of 1894–5. The second is an idealised picture of Togo's flagship 'Mikasa' and the Japanese battlefleet sweeping to victory at Tsushima, 27 May 1905.

and Japanese ambitions came into conflict, and war broke out in 1904 when Japanese ships attacked the Russian base without warning. Though Russia was so big, the Japanese had a stronger fleet in those seas, and this let them pour troops into Korea and Manchuria while the Russians had to bring their reinforcements thousands of miles by a railway which was mainly single-track. There were great battles with enormous casualties, for this was the first major war in which big guns with high-explosive shells, machine guns and magazine rifles were fully used – it was in every way the first twentieth-century war. The Russians were defeated. In an attempt to win control of the sea, Russia sent her Baltic fleet round the world; when it reached the Straits of Tsushima the Japanese fleet destroyed it. Peace was made in 1905 with the Russians retiring to Siberia, leaving Japan to dominate Korea and North China – she annexed Korea in 1910.

In half a century from being forced to admit the first Westerners, Japan had become the equal of the great European powers. But would those powers now accept her as an equal, and was Japan genuinely becoming Western in her outlook? During the Russo–Japanese War, almost all the European powers sympathised with Russia; whatever their previous differences, whites ought to hold together against yellows. Britain, though, signed an alliance with Japan – like her, a small group of islands off the shores of a continent that was not always friendly, and like her protecting herself with sea power.

4 The Western giant

The U.S.A. grasps her destiny

Two of the powers that had helped to prise open the Far East were Russia and the U.S.A. The Russians had come a great distance across land, the Americans across the Pacific Ocean. But even while sending her ships across the ocean, the U.S.A. was also expanding across the great land mass that lay next to her.

As soon as the U.S.A. had bought Louisiana (page 5) people began to move into that land. Later in the century an American writer referred, in words that became famous, to 'our manifest destiny to overspread the continent allotted by Providence for the free development of our yearly multiplying millions'. Already many people in the U.S.A. believed that the whole of North America was theirs.

In 1804–6 President Jefferson sent a small party led by Meriwether Lewis and William Clarke to try to find a way across the continent. Enduring great difficulties, but without fighting, they crossed vast plains and high mountain ranges to reach the Pacific in what was known as the Oregon Country, which the U.S.A. now claimed. A few fur trappers made their way here, and others came to trap in the Rockies. These were soon known as the 'mountain men' who lived like Red Indians, only they were more solitary; they preferred to live alone in the wilds, rarely returning to some trading post to sell their furs and buy powder and shot. These trappers had turned their backs on settled life but, though they had no wish to do so, they were exploring paths by which settlers soon came spreading after them.

Some trading companies built forts along the trails. Some

The three forks of the Missouri in Montana, seen from upstream. Lewis looked at this scene from the cliff at the bottom left of the picture, and the country was still in its natural state when A. E. Mathews made this drawing in 1867.

A pioneer farmstead, painted by John Halkett in 1822. It looks rough but not miserable. The nearby trees have been killed by ringing and burning, but not yet felled; there is a fairly extensive clearing behind the house.

parties of farmers, hearing of the fertility of the land by the Pacific, followed the Oregon Trail across the centre of the continent and settled in the far north-west, joining the fur traders and missionaries who were already well established there in the 1830s and 1840s. But the main tide of settlement, naturally, was the spread of parties of hopeful would-be farmers westwards from the existing states. These people faced a hard life, hacking out small rough plots and trying to work them up to large farms. Often they remained very much as they began, struggling to make a living in backwoods conditions. It was this pioneer life, though, that later writers believed to have given a special quality to American character.

The pioneers were sometimes from the settled states near the Atlantic coast, but many of them in the first part of the nineteenth century were immigrants from north-western Europe, mainly the British Isles. It could be assumed that these were people who were failures in their home countries, but equally it could be claimed that they were the most enter-

left: *Where the Laramie and North Platte rivers join, in what is now Wyoming, fur traders built a log fort in 1834. It was named Fort William, but usually called Fort Laramie. This painting of it was made in 1837 by A. J. Miller. It became an important trade centre, a halt on the Oregon Trail and a stage for the Pony Express and Overland Stage coaches.*

right: *Cerro Gordo, Sunday morning, 18 April 1847; the Americans storm an important pass on the road from the coast to Mexico City. This is an example of the cheap prints that gave a lot of people at the time their ideas of what a battle was like. In fact, it is probably no more than a scene of colourful violence imagined by a rather bad artist – it even looks as if the soldiers with the Stars and Stripes are being repulsed from the position where the Eagle and Serpent flag flies.*

prising. The pioneer had to be hard-working, resourceful and tough. He was a realist. He did not esteem others for their social airs and graces or their aristocratic blood, but for what they could do and what they had achieved. On the frontier everyone had an equal chance, nobody had privileges. This, it has been argued, made the U.S.A. a country of equality and opportunity.

The first president to represent this sort of attitude is said to have been Andrew Jackson, who was in power from 1829 to 1837. Before him, the leaders of the U.S.A. had been men like Washington and Jefferson, educated as gentlemen. Jackson's brand of democracy was more down-to-earth, and one of its features was that strength and success got the rewards. For instance, the party that won an election was entitled to reward its supporters with official jobs. And people who stood in the way of the growth of the U.S.A. must be removed.

This meant the Red Indians. Jackson's policy was to have none of them east of the Mississippi. Perhaps this made sense if the Indians were still living a savage hunting life. However, some tribes had settled down and had taken successfully to living like white men, even to the buying of negro slaves to work on their farms. These were the so-called 'civilised tribes'. Their civilisation did not save them. The best-known case was that of the Cherokee tribe. The authorities of the state of Georgia claimed their lands. The Cherokees took the case to court, and won. So Jackson simply ordered them to leave their homes, and sent them to bleak lands to the west. On the journey and in their new home, many died of the hardships.

This same conviction, that the U.S.A. had a right to any lands geographically connected with its existing territory, took effect in other ways. The attempts to seize Canada in the 1812 war failed, but in 1819 the U.S. government took advantage of Spain's difficulties in South America to force her to sell Florida. It was not from an old imperial power, however, but from a fellow American republic that the U.S.A. gained a really enormous increase in territory. Mexico in the 1830s and 1840s was badly ruled, and this provided opportunities and excuses. First came Texan independence. Texas was a huge province on the north-east of Mexico. It had a small, scattered population, and many American settlers had moved in. These people declared Texas to be an independent republic in 1836, and beat off Mexican attempts to regain control. In 1845 Texas joined the U.S.A. In 1846 the U.S. government, wanting to add New Mexico, brought about a war with Mexico. As expected, the Mexican army was very badly led, and the result was complete victory for the U.S. army, which occupied Mexico City. By the Treaty of Guadalupe Hidalgo in 1848 Mexico gave up not only New Mexico but also all the lands westwards from there to the Pacific, including California. It was a gain comparable with the Louisiana Purchase, and gave the U.S.A.

the whole continent, from ocean to ocean, in a broad belt somewhat wider than the north-south breadth of the thirteen original states.

There was already an accepted method of dealing with new lands, which had been worked out early in the century. At first the land would be classed as a territory under the federal government. When the population grew large enough, it could be recognised as a state and join the union as a full member. Thus, as people moved westwards into the new lands, gradually the number of states in the U.S.A. increased; each new state was added as a star to the flag, but the number of stripes remained thirteen.

Now the U.S.A. seemed well set to growing, to filling out the land she had seized. Just before the Treaty of Guadalupe Hidalgo gold had been discovered in California, and the first modern gold rush began. From Europe and from the eastern states would-be miners came in their thousands, some all the way by ship, others by wagon across the great plains and through the mountains. They became famous as the Forty-Niners, but after 1849, when hopes of quick fortunes had passed away, these people and their descendants found that California was a very rich and pleasant land. Its fertility, climate and size eventually made it one of the most important states in the union.

The U.S.A. was not merely growing territorially, it was also growing industrially. The inventive enterprise of Fulton and Whitney (see page 5) was carried on by generations of American inventors. Between 1830 and 1860 the U.S.A. was the birthplace of reaping machines and steel ploughs, revolvers and sewing machines, vulcanised rubber and the electric telegraph. Railways were built fast, and began to bind the great diverse country together. At sea the American *Savannah* in 1819 was the first steam-aided ship to cross the Atlantic, and in the middle of the century, though steam was becoming yearly more important, Yankee clippers were still among the fastest ships afloat. Perhaps it was impossible that so great a space could ever become overcrowded, yet in some places, mainly in the northern states, populations were crowding together in industrial centres where the factories and foundries were as big as anything in the industrialised parts of Europe. And the United States were obviously going to grow far greater.

'The Centennial Mirror', published in St Louis in 1876, tried to show the changes that had taken place during the hundred years since the Declaration of Independence. Besides such big innovations as steamships and farm machinery there are little things such as sewing machines and paraffin lamps. Americans did not claim to have invented them all, but they prided themselves on being quick to make use of new ideas.

The American Civil War

As the U.S.A. grew a gap opened between two groups of states and became steadily wider. The industries, the big towns and the expanding population were mainly in the northern states. The southern states still lived mainly by agriculture, and the characteristic farm was a plantation, growing cotton and worked by black slaves. Wealthy plantation-owners prided themselves on being gentlemen of culture, and their houses were frequently dignified mansions with a strong air of the elegance of the old regime. Men of this class had taken the lead, naturally, in the U.S. Congress and became officers in the army. But by the middle of the century their leadership was being eroded by politicians from northern states.

The southerners disliked the Yankees, as the northerners were called. They accused them of being brash, greedy, vulgar and often dishonest. The Yankees said that the boasted southern culture was based on degradation and cruelty, on slavery, and they also pointed to all those southern whites who were not aristocratic planters. The 'poor whites' sometimes lived in worse poverty than the slaves, and the 'hill-billies' in their remote cabins had a reputation for brutish ignorance. Southerners retorted that workers in northern factories were often treated far worse than the slaves on southern plantations, and

'Black and White Slaves', published in New York in 1844. It seems to be showing how much better the U.S.A. is than Britain, but really it is propaganda for the southern states against the northern, for the Christian gentleman against the cruelly selfish industrialist. The following lines were printed above the pictures.

America
God bless you massa! you feed and clothe us. When we are sick you nurse us, and when too old to work, you provide for us!

These poor creatures are a sacred legacy from my ancestors and while a dollar is left me, nothing shall be spared to increase their comfort and happiness.

England
Oh heaven! in this boasted land of freedom to be starving for want of employment! No relief from the purse-proud aristocracy whose bloated fortunes have been made by our blood and toil!

Come pack off to the work house! that's the only fit asylum for you!

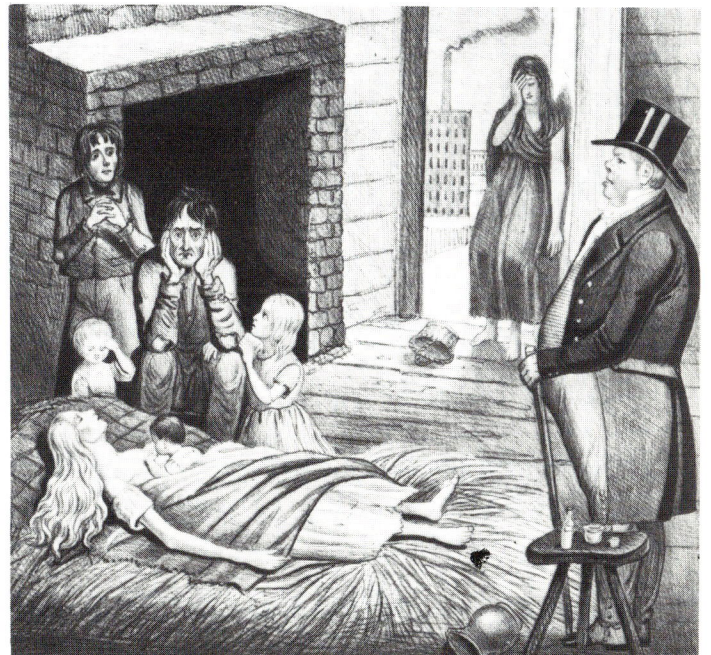

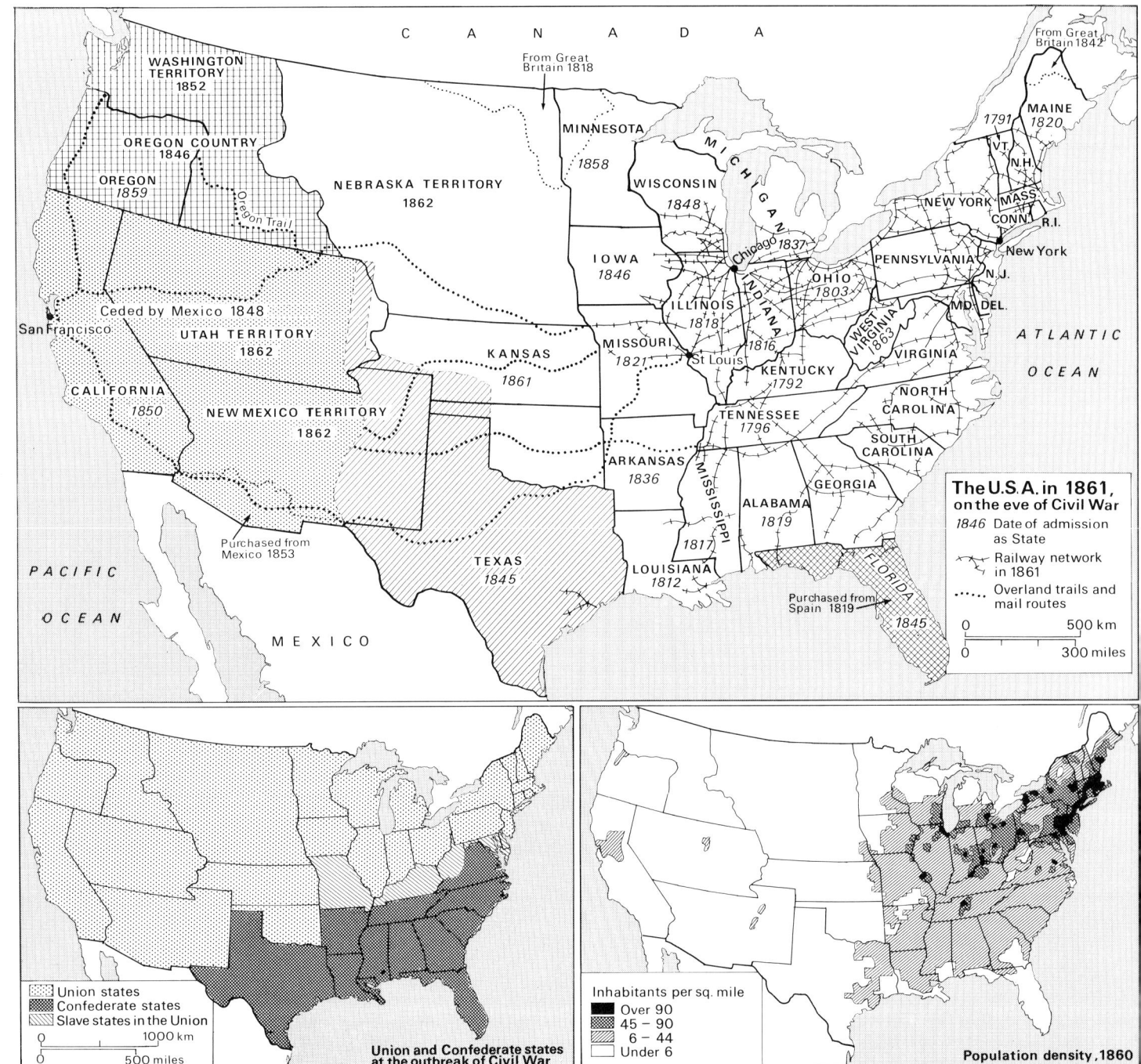

Two New York recruiting posters. The first makes a direct appeal in terms of money and good conditions, but it also has a symbolic picture: on one side is the sunny, thriving town that the soldiers are leaving, on the other the war-torn Southern countryside, and in the centre a Federal zouave triumphantly holds aloft the Stars and Stripes over a vanquished foe who has fallen across the Confederate Stars and Bars flag. The other poster appeals to men who fled to the U.S.A. after the collapse of the 1848–9 revolutions in Europe.

it was hypocritical for Yankees to criticise the south. Indeed, they feared that northerners were going to use their growing control over Congress to alter the import and export regulations so as to favour the north's industries at the expense of the south's trade in raw materials. Distrust and hostility mounted.

The differences between the two societies came to a head in the argument over slavery. Slavery was not forbidden by the Constitution. It was for each state to allow it or forbid it; northern states opted to be 'free', southern states to keep their 'peculiar institution' of negro slavery. In the north a powerful movement grew up, urging that slavery was an abominable offence in the eyes of God and man, and ought to be abolished. The 'abolitionists' held meetings, published books and newspaper articles – *Uncle Tom's Cabin* was their best-seller – and organised a secret system of helping slaves to escape from the south which was nicknamed the 'underground railroad'. Southerners denied the stories of cruelty, and accused the abolitionists of being religious cranks and troublemakers. Men like John Brown, they rightly pointed out, were murderous fanatics; but, when Brown tried to raise armed rebellion and was hanged for it, many Yankees thought of him as a noble Christian martyr. As new states were admitted to the union there was furious debate about whether or not they should forbid slavery; in Kansas the violence almost reached the scale of a war, and the territory was called 'bleeding Kansas'.

Could any country survive, split by so bitter a quarrel? Some southerners thought that it was impossible. And they saw the north steadily growing stronger. They pointed out that the U.S.A. was not one state, but a union of many, and said that each state had the right to withdraw, or secede. They urged their states to secede from the federation and to form another group, a confederacy. In late 1860 the first states began to secede and by the spring of 1861 all the south had withdrawn from the union. These states called themselves the Confederate States of America, the C.S.A.

The man who had to face this challenge was the newly

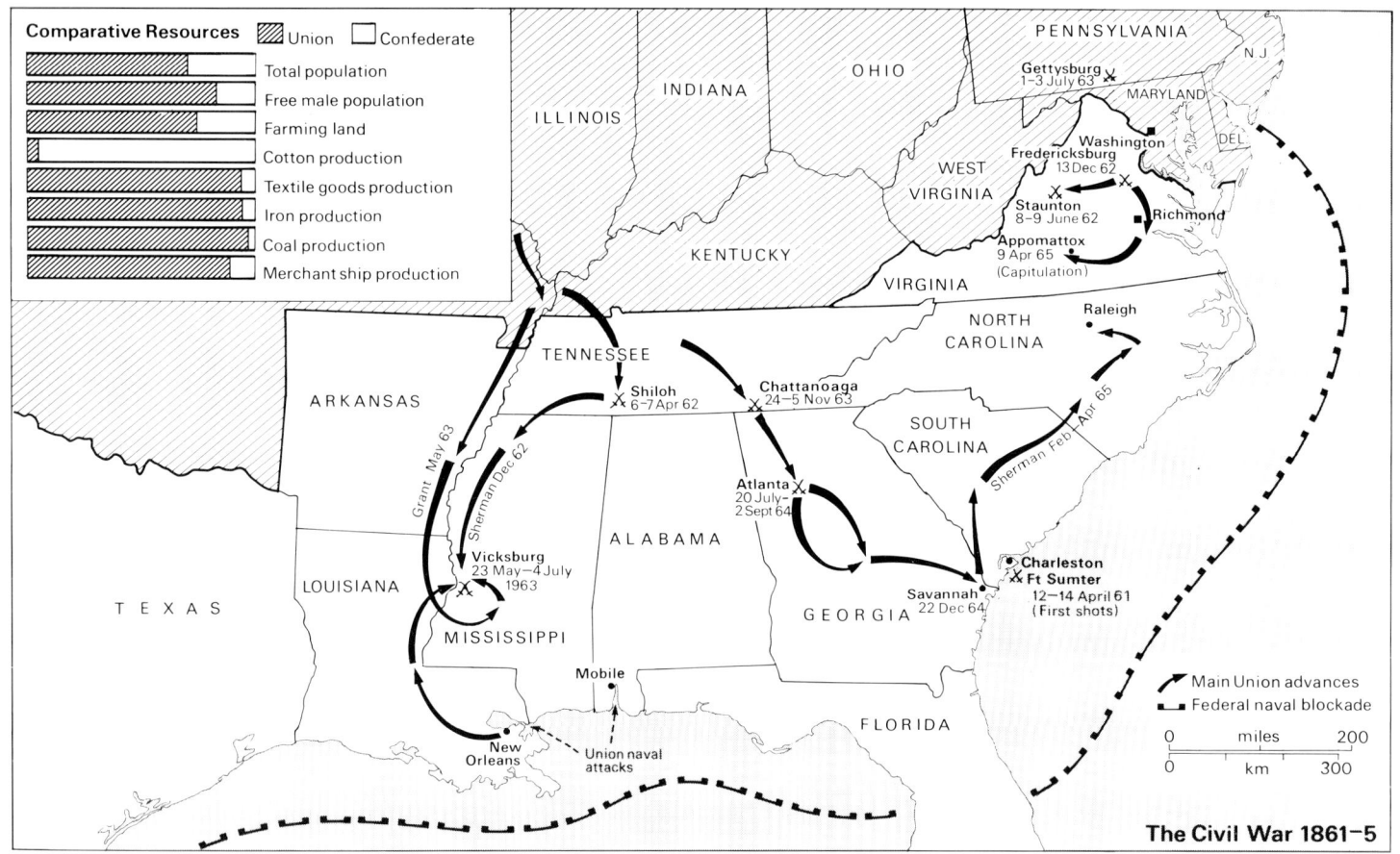

elected president of the U.S.A., Abraham Lincoln. Was he to accept that the Constitution meant that in the last resort each state was sovereign, and could go its own way? Or was he to say that the U.S.A. was one country, and that to attempt to take parts away from it was treason? Lincoln and most northern leaders said that the union was sacred and that it must be maintained, by force if necessary. Lincoln was in a very difficult situation. He was a country lawyer from Illinois, which had still been frontier when he was a boy. He was very tall, clumsy-looking, and sometimes gave the impression of being an oaf; his enemies – and there were many of these in the more polished set of politicians and politicians' wives in Washington D.C. – referred to him as 'the gorilla'. His friends said that beneath the awkward surface there was a very shrewd

mind, a humane heart and a firm spirit. He needed all three. He was very clear on what the war was about. It was not about slavery. It was about saving the union. He said that if he could save the union by freeing the slaves, he would do so; and that if he could save it by keeping slavery, he would do so. But it was too late. The U.S. government would have to fight to hold the south.

Both sides had to raise armies almost from nothing. The old U.S. regular army was very small, and many of its officers were southerners who decided that their first loyalty lay with their states. Some of them were very reluctant. Robert E. Lee, for example, could have accepted high command in the Federal army, and he was against slavery; but he was a Virginian, and felt that he must serve Virginia first. So the Confederacy got the officer who soon became their most famous and best-loved general.

The Confederates selected Richmond, Virginia, as their capital. It was challengingly near the Federal capital. But nobody expected a long struggle. Confederates thought the Federals would soon give up when they saw that the whole south was against them; it really was not worth struggling to force the southerners to become fellow-citizens against their will. Many Federals thought that the rebellion, as they called it, was mostly hot air, and that a few shots would disperse it. In fact the war lasted four years and cost 234,000 lives in battle and another 388,000 from disease and hardship.

The main fighting took place in two theatres of war. One was the area between Washington and Richmond, where Lee and his Army of Northern Virginia fought a ding-dong war against the Federal Army of the Potomac, usually bigger and better-armed but not so well led. Despite all the battles, neither side was able to win a decisive advantage. The other theatre was the western one, along the Mississippi. After two years of hard fighting the Federals won control of the whole river, cutting the western Confederate states off from the rest.

The Confederates went on fighting, harder than ever as the Federals grew stronger. The Federal commanders decided that nothing but sheer destruction would bring the Confederates to surrender. So, while General Grant hammered at Lee in continual frontal attacks, General Sherman marched from the Mississippi theatre to the Atlantic coast, destroying everything that lay in his path as he cut his way through the state of Georgia. He said: 'War is hell', and he worked on the principle that it was best to face this hard truth and so finish more quickly. The south never forgave the march through Georgia, but it may have won the war for the Federals. Lee, with Sherman behind him and Grant in front, had to surrender on 9 April 1865, and the remaining Confederate forces had to do the same within the next few weeks. The Confederate soldiers had fought well, but in the end the superior numbers and wealth of the Federals crushed them.

Now what were the victors to do? This was not the sort of war that could be ended by a treaty and the yielding of a few square miles of territory. The whole of the defeated power had to be made once more part of the victorious power. Lincoln thought long about the problem as victory drew near. He had

Colonel Hall attacks General Pickett's Confederates as they attempted to take the ridge held by the Union army near Gettysburg in 1863. Pickett's men were decimated and had to retreat. The charge has been called the high tide of the Confederacy. The drawing is by A. R. Waud.

President Lincoln with generals of the Army of the Potomac photographed in October 1862 at Antietam. The American Civil War is the first to be well recorded in photographs, for there were by this time many professional photographers in the U.S.A. The best known was Mathew Brady, who took this photograph.

Another Federal statesman, as seen by Southern sympathisers after the war!

already come to the conclusion that slavery would have to end, and in 1863 it was declared illegal in the rebel states; two years later the thirteenth amendment to the Constitution prohibited slavery anywhere in the U.S.A. Apart from this, Lincoln wanted to be friendly to the south, to help to repair the damage as soon as possible and to persuade the ex-Confederates to become good citizens of the union they had fought against so furiously. On 14 April 1865 Lincoln was shot by a Confederate sympathiser and died next day. The men who succeeded him did not believe in being soft towards the south.

The politicians and officials who moved into the ex-Confederate states behind the Federal soldiers in order to supervise what the government called its Reconstruction policy soon earned the reputation of wanting to punish and humiliate the beaten rebels. Ex-Confederates were not allowed to take any part in politics, but ex-slaves were. In some southern states everything was controlled by a few Yankees supported by large numbers of blacks, the Yankees being corrupt or fanatical, the blacks being ignorant. This, at least, was what southerners came to believe as they bitterly thought of their ruined plantations and towns and their lost power. The Reconstruction was certainly not as wicked as they said, but there were bad cases of corruption and there were northerners who used their opportunities to plunder and insult the conquered.

The people who suffered most for this were the ex-slaves. Secret societies were formed to punish blacks who forgot their place, and these groups became the Ku Klux Klan. With their white hoods and robes and their fantastic titles, the Klansmen may have seemed to some people childish and absurd, but black people learned to fear them for the beatings and killings they perpetrated, and many white southerners looked on them as heroes. After a few years the U.S. government began to restore to the ex-Confederate states their former rights. The whites once again could elect and be elected to state governments, and blacks who had been in office were all rapidly voted out. Then the southern state governments began to make rules and regulations against the negroes. They could not enslave them again, nor deprive them of their rights as U.S. citizens, but they could ensure that they were kept apart from whites and were the last to receive any benefits. They got the poorest education and the worst jobs. Even the poorest white could look down on the blacks.

So the southern states slowly and painfully began to recover from the war, still showing livid scars. Meanwhile the rest of the U.S.A. was forging ahead.

Filling the west

In the thirty years after the war the U.S.A. spread over the vast empty space that lay within its frontiers and had so far been left mainly to the countless herds of bison and to the Indians that followed and lived off them. In the earlier part of the century the great plains had not seemed very attractive and profitable – they were sometimes called the Great American Desert. But in the later part they became valuable. Cattle became big business.

As we have seen, settlements were gradually extending westwards, and cities were growing. The population of the U.S.A. was increasing fast, and had to be fed. Railways could be built quickly to carry food to where it was needed. The prairies were free – mile after mile of grazing where cattle could be reared. And so the great days of cattle ranching began.

On the open ranges the cattle would be herded by the cowboys, herdsmen who had copied the skills, equipment and even the name of the Mexican *vaqueros*. When the animals were ready for market, the cowboys had to take them there. This often meant driving immense herds for hundreds of miles across wild country, where, apart from natural dangers, they had to risk attack from outlaws or unfriendly Indians. At last they would reach the nearest railhead, and could load the cattle to go by train on the final stage of their journey to the slaughterhouses of the great cities, especially Chicago. It was a rough life for the cowboys, and they had little pay and less to spend it on. At the railheads there were settlements to handle the business of the cattle, and there were also plenty of saloons where the cowboys could drink and gamble away what they had earned, and sometimes get killed. Places like Abilene would be notorious for a few years while they were flourishing railheads, and then the railway and the trade would move on, and they would become quiet little towns.

One reason for the many killings was that these men were very well armed. They had to be, to protect themselves while doing their job, and there were new weapons that allowed them to blaze away several shots at a time. Revolvers and repeating rifles were temptingly easy to use.

Meanwhile railways were crossing the prairies, partly to connect new settlements with the eastern states, partly to link with the Pacific coast. In 1869 the Union Pacific Railway was completed, from ocean to ocean. Along these railway lines

The Douglas Knox ranch in Idaho, painted by an unknown artist in 1882. This fertile country lay farther west than the great plains and the Rocky Mountains, next to Oregon.

Abilene, Kansas, from a drawing made about 1870. The railway, with the telegraph line beside it, drives straight across the endlessly flat plain, but here are the big stockyards where the cattle trail meets the railway.

A buffalo shoot on the Kansas–Pacific railway as shown in an illustrated newspaper of 1871. Though it may seem unlikely that animals came as close as this to the train and the hunters, there is no doubt that luxuriously equipped sporting expeditions were arranged by the rail companies, and the slaughter of bison was immense.

farms and small towns began to grow. The land was being criss-crossed with iron tracks and speckled with settlements.

All this meant death to the Plains Indians. The tribes had not been worried by the earliest wagon trains making trails to the west. Sometimes they had demanded gifts, but they usually let them through. But as more whites used the trails, the Indians began to be suspicious and sometimes hostile. Then came the cattle ranches, interfering with the Indians' freedom to wander and hunt. This was a serious threat to their way of life. But the railways were fatal. They made barriers across the plains so that the herds of bison and their hunters could no longer move freely. The railway companies also employed riflemen to slaughter the bison in order to feed the gangs of navvies building the railways, and these men, with their modern weapons, massacred the animals by the thousand so that the Indians could see their food supply dwindling. The railways even brought sportsmen from the eastern states and from Europe to shoot the bison for mere amusement. The Indians tried to protect their food supplies.

This was one of the main reasons behind the increase in fighting between red and white men, but there were all sorts of other reasons for particular outbreaks. Perhaps the U.S. government failed to keep settlers off land that it had guaranteed to an Indian tribe, because it was found to be valuable. Perhaps whites were attacked in time of peace by braves who did not feel bound by whatever treaty the local chief had made – they might not even belong to the same tribe. There were many savage little wars. Rarely the Indians won a victory, by far the most famous being when the Sioux wiped out Colonel Custer and his entire command in 1876. Usually the superior discipline and weapons of the U.S. army gave them victory. By the 1890s all surviving Indians had been swept into tribal reservations where they lived partly on the charity of the U.S. government, and the great centre of the continent was being worked by the white men.

The cowboys did not last much longer than the Indians. There came other white men to share the open range. In some places sheep farmers, in other places settlers trying to raise crops. Some of them fenced off land with a simple new invention that proved to be the cowboy's worst enemy: barbed wire. Artesian wells made land that had once been fit only for grazing fertile enough for corn. More people kept moving in, states were created, law and order was more firmly enforced. By the end of the century, there were still wide open spaces and big ranches, but the Wild West was finished. It was a legendary period, even at its height, thanks partly to the efforts of newspapermen and showmen like Ned Buntline and Buffalo Bill Cody, who stirred the imagination of the stay-at-homes in the eastern states and Europe. But it lasted for barely thirty years.

The land of opportunity

The thousands of settlers who flowed into the west needed every sort of manufacture in exchange for their beef and corn, and the factories of the east expanded to supply them. Unlike other new white nations growing outside Europe, the U.S.A. did not have to import its textiles and hardware. Within its borders most of the minerals needed in industry were discovered in great quantities. The growth of industries and business empires in the U.S.A. that went on while the west was being occupied was probably much more important, employed far more people and was, in its way, just as hard and violent as the Wild West. For men with ambition and ability there were bigger fortunes to be won in the east than in the west.

Some great fortunes were made in the earlier part of the century, like that of 'Commodore' Vanderbilt who started as a coastal sailor, fought his way to controlling fleets of merchant

William Frederick Cody, 1846–1917, was a Pony Express rider, army scout and Indian fighter and bison hunter on the grand scale. Ned Buntline made him the hero of one of his adventure stories in 1870, and in 1872 persuaded him to act in Wild West plays. Soon 'Buffalo Bill' had his own company, putting on specially written plays; this is an advertisement.

Part of the supply base for General Grant's army at City Point, Virginia, in 1864, photographed by Mathew Brady or one of his assistants. It gives a slight idea of the material that had to be bought. At one relatively small battle, Stone's River/Murfreesboro on 31 December 1862, the Federal artillery is reported to have fired 20,307 rounds and the infantry more than 2,000,000 rounds. The war cost the Federal government about two million dollars per day, and a good deal of this was profit for businessmen.

ships and eventually made his millions out of the new railways. Then the war gave a wonderful opportunity to ambitious businessmen. The government needed weapons and equipment of all kinds in quantities that had never been dreamed of before, and it wanted them fast. Wartime contractors have had a bad name in many periods of history, but probably never deserved it more than during the American Civil War. Government officials could be tricked or bribed, and so could politicians, by the men who supplied the soldiers with guns that would not shoot straight, boots made chiefly of paper and meat that was rotten.

After the war, expecially during the presidency of the wartime hero Grant from 1869 to 1877, corruption on a vast scale was revealed. Grant himself was not involved, but he was careless and too trusting. His brother-in-law was in a plot to use government powers to get control of all the gold in the U.S.A.; Grant woke up in time to stop this, but the result was a financial collapse that ruined thousands of innocent people who had invested their money in firms that now went bankrupt. Crédit Mobilier was an even worse scandal. This was the name of the company that built the Union Pacific Railway. The railway company received big sums of government money and paid them to Crédit Mobilier, which overcharged. The extra profit went to the Crédit Mobilier shareholders, who happened to be the very Union Pacific men who had paid the government money to Crédit Mobilier, together with leading politicians. Even the Vice-President of the U.S.A. was involved. Few of the guilty were punished, and most were allowed to pretend innocence. Cases like these – and they were not rare – eventually led to tighter laws being made and enforced, to limit some of the 'sharper' ways of doing business. In the meantime there were plenty of opportunities for clever men to make huge fortunes without actually breaking the law.

One of the most remarkable, and a splendid example for those who came to think of the U.S.A. as a land where anyone with the right qualities could rise 'from rags to riches', was Andrew Carnegie. He came from Scotland at the age of thirteen in 1848 – his father was a Chartist who emigrated when the movement finally collapsed. He began work with a railway company, and his employers noticed his keenness and intelligence. They promoted him rapidly, and he became one of the chief men of the company in his early twenties. When the war broke out, Carnegie became convinced that the demand for steel was going to continue and grow, and that this was the time to get into the industry. He had no technical knowledge, but he had wonderful shrewdness in negotiating business

Andrew Carnegie, 1835–1919. The portrait is from one of the medals awarded by a fund he set up in 1904 in the U.S.A. and 1908 in Britain to reward brave deeds.

above: *The cottage in Dunfermline, Fife, where Carnegie was born.*

below: *One of the best-known of the Carnegie charities was the building and equipping of libraries. This is the first Carnegie Library, built at Braddock, Pennsylvania in 1889; the watercolour was probably painted then.*

deals. He bought his way into one or two companies at first, and then more, and still more. When he was sixty-five he retired and spent the rest of his life giving money to what he judged to be good causes. At this time his companies, now called the United States Steel Corporation, produced two-thirds of all the steel made in the U.S.A.

John D. Rockefeller became even richer. He was the son of a self-styled 'doctor' who travelled from town to town like a showman, selling 'medicines' that he had concocted. Young John moved to Cleveland, Ohio, and joined a small business partnership when he was eighteen. Two years later, in 1859, he was recognised as one of the ablest businessmen in the town, and when the others wanted somebody to go and find out about prospects in western Pennsylvania, where oil was being produced, they sent him. Oil from natural seepage had been used for some time, but in 1859 the world's first oil well was drilled, and gushed at the rate of twenty-five barrels a day. What steel was to Carnegie, oil was to Rockefeller. He was not

right: *John Davison Rockefeller, 1839–1937, at the age of 41.*

below: *A newspaper cartoon of 1884 shows the tentacles of Standard Oil seizing everything – with one tentacle very close to the Capitol in the distance.*

the only man to see the possibilities, but nobody else in the industry could match his shrewdness in business deals. Also he picked brilliant partners and assistants. So his company, Standard Oil, became one of the biggest oil firms in the U.S.A. But Rockefeller was not content. Why not the biggest of all? Why not the only one? If all the oil companies were to combine in one group, they would save the money that they now spent in competing against each other and could fix the price of oil at whatever they thought best. Such a group was given the name of a *trust*. Rockefeller persuaded or forced one company after another to join Standard Oil until he had a trust which practically held the monopoly of all oil in the U.S.A.

Rockefeller may have been the greatest, but there were many others who built up businesses that gave them enormous wealth and economic power. To some Americans it seemed that these men had more power to affect the lives of people in the U.S.A., and in other countries too, than all the politicians and generals put together. But when there were attempts to make new laws to reduce the powers of the big companies, there were always other Americans who argued that in a free country people should be allowed to do what they wished with

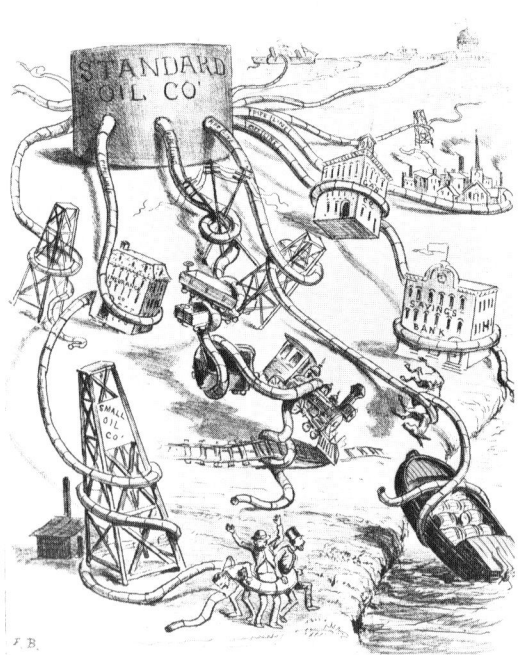

right: One of the most important groups of immigrants was the Irish, who came in especially large numbers after the Potato Famine of the 1840s. This picture of Irish immigrants landing at the Battery, New York, was painted in 1855 by Samuel B. Waugh.

below left: In Chicago in 1886 a strike led to a riot in which people were killed. Anarchists seized the opportunity and held a meeting in Haymarket Square on 4 May. The speakers called for revolution, the police moved in, somebody threw a bomb, and seven policemen were mortally injured. The bomb-thrower was never found, but seven anarchists were condemned to death on the grounds that they had openly encouraged such violence, and four were executed. This drawing of the bombing appeared in 'Harper's Weekly', 15 May 1886.

their own property, and that it was the driving force of these millionaires that brought wealth to the whole country.

Such arguments sounded hollow to many of the thousands of people who kept the mines and mills and railways and factories running. If there was incredible wealth at the top there was intolerable poverty at the bottom. Employers tried to save money by keeping wages down, while their workers could read in the newspapers about the profits these same businesses were making. Some of the industrial towns were even dirtier and more depressing than anything in Europe; a distinguished British writer who was a guest of Carnegie's said, after seeing some of the towns near Pittsburgh where Carnegie's iron-workers lived, that a month in such a place would justify suicide. Employers, on the whole, did not feel any responsibility. In business it was every man for himself. When workers tried to form unions, most employers tried to prevent it by dismissing workers who joined. There was violence on both sides. In 1877 a widespread rail strike led to arson, murders and pitched battles between troops and armed strikers; soldiers had to be withdrawn from fighting the Sioux to restore order in Chicago. In 1892, during a dispute at the Homestead ironworks, Carnegie's company brought in 300 armed men from the Pinkerton detective agency; after a day's fighting in which 14 were killed and 163 wounded on both sides, the 'Pinks' surrendered, but the company got the better of the dispute in the end.

Still the freedom, the space, the chance to earn a better living or, with luck, a fortune, attracted more and more immigrants to the U.S.A. Many still came from the British Isles, but a growing proportion was arriving from other parts of Europe, from Italy, Germany, Scandinavia, and from Poland and other provinces of the Russian Empire. They set a serious problem to the U.S. government. They were wanted to fill the country and to enrich it with their work, but they often did not speak English and they often had been brought up in societies with very different conventions and beliefs. Sometimes they tended to settle beside others who had come from their old countries, and to continue with the speech and traditions of the lands they had left. Could all these people be brought to see themselves first and foremost as members of a new nation?

All U.S. citizens were expected to speak the official language, English. They were expected to learn about the

Constitution and to accept the ideals of the heroes of 1776. The sacred symbol was the flag; at school every morning children were taught to stand, hand on heart, in salute to the Stars and Stripes.

Aggressive patriotism was not new in the U.S.A., as the record of expansion in the earlier part of the century showed. The immense achievements, the energy and growth of the later part of the century added reasons for pride. Foreigners often accused Americans of being boastful and over confident, but there was some excuse. In a century the U.S.A. had grown from being a bunch of revolted colonies into one of the biggest and most powerful nations in the world. It was European. In one sense it was a second Europe, as the people were a mixture of so many different sorts of Europeans. Yet Americans still felt distrust of the old states of Europe that they had come from, and tried to keep clear of any entanglement in their futile discords and alliances.

Like other strong national groups, the Irish Americans did not forget their traditions; this contemporary picture shows the St Patrick's Day parade in New York, 1874. Groups like this were forces to be reckoned with in American politics.

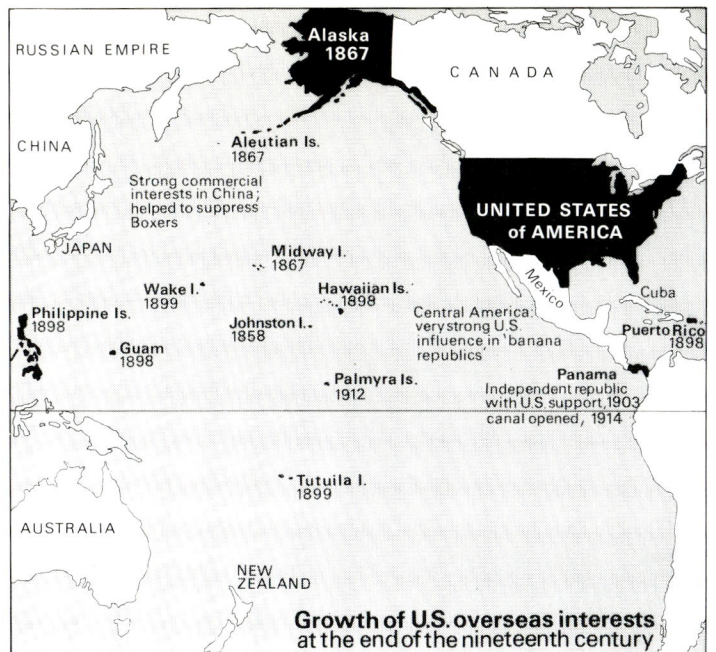

Growth of U.S. overseas interests at the end of the nineteenth century

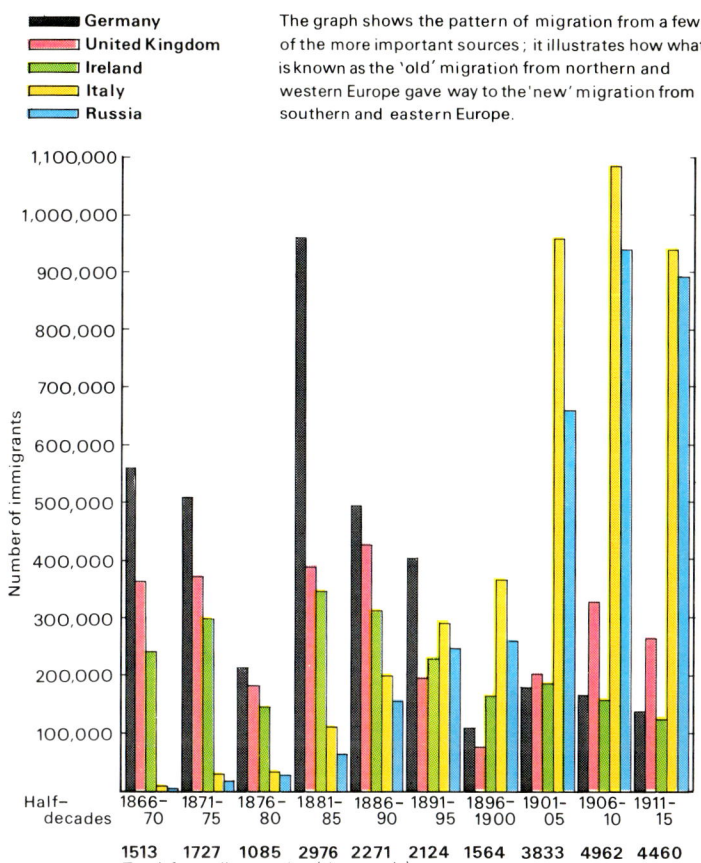

Immigration into the United States of America between the Civil War and the First World War

- Germany
- United Kingdom
- Ireland
- Italy
- Russia

The graph shows the pattern of migration from a few of the more important sources; it illustrates how what is known as the 'old' migration from northern and western Europe gave way to the 'new' migration from southern and eastern Europe.

The U.S.A. herself, though, had now grown to be a power with interests that led her into policies very like the imperialism of the old European powers. North American businessmen came to control more and more of the commerce and the industries of the Spanish-American republics, and the U.S. government was usually ready to threaten or to send ships and troops if the local people failed to pay what they owed. It was Porfirio Díaz, a president who had himself allowed U.S. and other foreign businessmen enormous influence in Mexico, who sighed: 'Poor Mexico! So far from God, so near to the United States!' Cynics now saw the Monroe Doctrine as meaning that the U.S.A. would keep the whole New World safe from everybody but herself. In 1898 the U.S.A. forced war on Spain, ostensibly for the sake of Cubans who wanted to be independent; in fact, war fever had been stirred up by newspapers, especially those controlled by W. R. Hearst. After a quick and easy victory the U.S.A. ensured that Cuba became independent, but took as her reward the islands of Puerto Rico, Guam and the Philippines. Many Filipinos had hoped for independence, and rose in revolt; it took three years for an army of 60,000 to enforce U.S. rule. The U.S.A. had already taken possession of the Hawaiian islands, which provided a useful naval base in the middle of the Pacific. She was now a world power.

There was one great hindrance to the development of American strength at sea: every ship sailing between the east and west coasts had to go round the southern tip of South America. There had been many plans to construct a canal across the isthmus of Panama, but it was U.S. wealth and technical skill that finally overcame the difficulties. The U.S. government obtained special rights from the republic of Panama, and opened the canal in August 1914.

5 The Eastern giant

The exploration of Siberia

Russian expansion eastwards seems to match and balance the westward expansion of the U.S.A., but there were big differences. The Russians were subjects of an autocratic emperor whose main interests lay elsewhere; they began more than two centuries before the Americans but they took much longer to settle the land.

The movement began in the sixteenth century, at the time when Tsars like Ivan the Terrible were turning the Principality of Moscow into the Russian Empire. Far to the north of Moscow, in the forested lands that stretched towards the White Sea, a family called Stroganoff had built up a highly successful business empire, supplying the cities further south with such products as honey and wax, salt and salt fish, and, by far the most valuable, furs. The Stroganoffs owned forts, stores, settlements; in practice, they were the rulers of that wide territory. But they depended on the goodwill of their Tsar. He found it advantageous to use them, and so he authorised the Stroganoffs to employ soldiers and to push their trading and hunting into the lands that lay beside and beyond the Ural Mountains, where animals with the most valuable furs were said to live.

People also lived there, but they were a sparse and weak population who could do little against the well-armed bands of Russians who came to demand furs. But there was, in the more

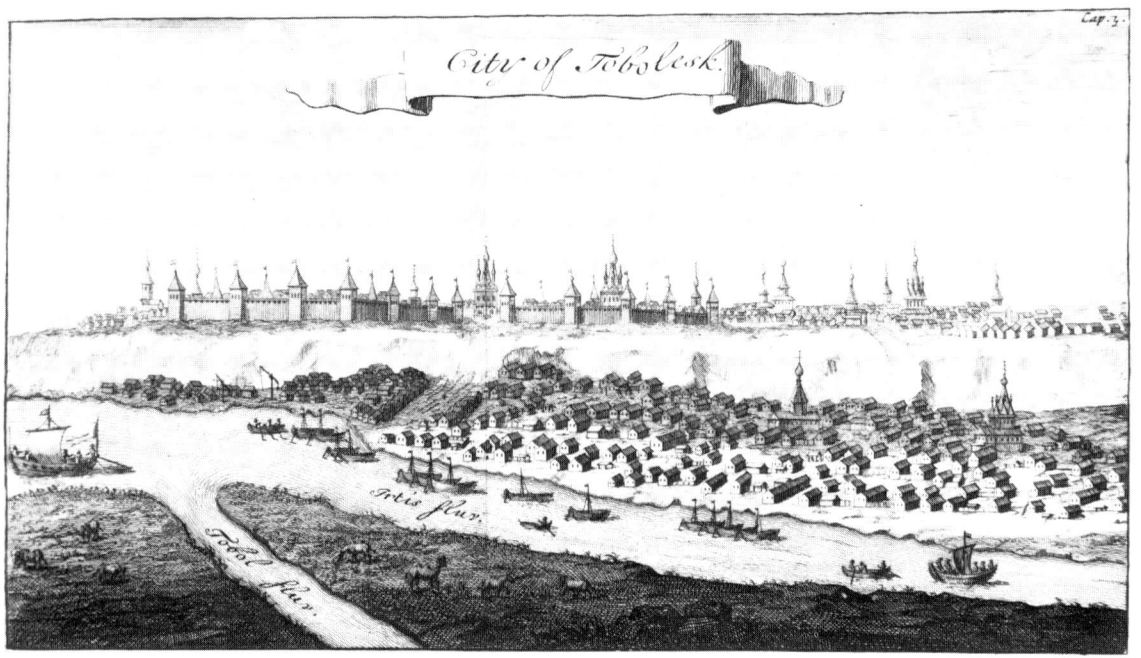

Tobolsk, the chief city of western Siberia, as shown in a travel book of 1705. It was built mainly of timber on a commanding site where the River Tobol joins the River Irtysh. Cossacks founded it in 1587, about 12 miles (19 km) from the capital of the khan they had defeated, and the kreml, or citadel, was built over a century later by Swedish prisoners-of-war.

This photograph, taken in May 1974 during the planning of the new Baikal–Amur railway, gives some impression of the way the vast Siberian forest, or taiga, covers the land. The view is at the confluence of the rivers Nia and Taura, and shows the taiga in spring; for most of the year it would be snow-clad.

southerly part of the land behind the Urals, a kingdom called Sibir ruled by a warlike khan. This was where there would be serious opposition. In 1581 the Stroganoffs sent several hundred men led by a Cossack named Yermak into Sibir. There were years of hard fighting, and Yermak himself was killed, but before his death he had proved that the land was very rich in furs and that the khan could be beaten. So the Tsar sent reinforcements and the khan fled. He himself had been an outsider, who had come with his men from the steppes of Central Asia, and the local tribesmen of Sibir had seen no reason to fight for him against the Russians. Thus only a few hundred Cossacks and soldiers were able to give Sibir to the Tsar.

But exactly what was Sibir? The khanate had stretched for a few hundred miles, with no very clear borders, and beyond that there seemed to be no more khans or kings, but a land of forests and plains and great rivers where the only humans were a few tribes of primitive hunters and fishers. While the Tsar's men set up forts and offices for governing Sibir, adventurers pushed into the wilderness that stretched eastwards.

These men were mostly Cossacks. The Cossacks were a frontier nation that had grown up during the sixteenth century on the plains that lay by the rivers Dnieper and Don, in the no-man's-land between Russians to the north and Tartars and Turks to the south. Many of them originally came from Russia, but they were a free people who might help the Tsar but were not his servants – unless, of course, he paid them. They lived by plundering Tartars and Turks; a Cossack was allowed to own herds of horses, but must never till the soil. They were proud of their freedom, of the dangerous life they led, and despised weakness or timidity.

The land beyond Sibir, the land we now know as Siberia, was immense, yet the Cossacks penetrated to its furthest limits in little more than half a century, and after them came a few traders and officials and soldiers who planted the Tsar's flag in remote settlements thousands of miles from Muscovy. Often the Cossacks found it best to travel by water, and built boats that carried them down the mighty rivers and sometimes even along the shores of the Arctic Ocean. So it was that a Cossack called Semyon Ivanovich Dezhnev in 1648 sailed round the eastern tip of Asia. At the time he got little credit. His report was filed in the nearest government office, at Yakutsk, and remained unknown until somebody went through the archives a century later.

By the 1650s some daring adventurers were on the River Amur, and here their career of depredation was at last halted when they encountered the frontier troops of the Chinese Empire. There had already been attempts by the Russian

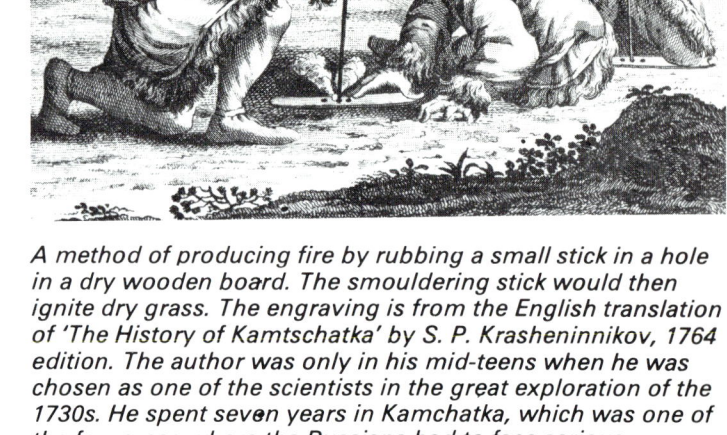

A method of producing fire by rubbing a small stick in a hole in a dry wooden board. The smouldering stick would then ignite dry grass. The engraving is from the English translation of 'The History of Kamtschatka' by S. P. Krasheninnikov, 1764 edition. The author was only in his mid-teens when he was chosen as one of the scientists in the great exploration of the 1730s. He spent seven years in Kamchatka, which was one of the few areas where the Russians had to face serious opposition from the natives.

left: *The restored corner tower of an* ostrog, *or fort, built by Cossacks in the late seventeenth century at Bratsk in the Baikal region.*

government to make agreements with China; the first envoy from Moscow reached Peking as early as 1618, after travelling through central Asia. But, as we have seen, the Chinese were not very interested. By treaties in 1689 and 1727 Russian representatives had to recognise the border between China and Siberia where the Chinese said it was. In return, China permitted a small amount of trade, which was useful to the settlers in places like Yakutsk and Irkutsk.

The Russians also stopped short of the steppes and the cities of central Asia, where both the nomad tribesmen and the soldiers of the emirs were capable of resisting the small Russian forces. The Tsars had not the resources to fight a real war so far away, and there was no reason why they should want to, anyway.

After Peter the Great had brought Russia more closely into contact with western Europe it became common for the Russian government to support scientific and technical enquiries and to employ foreign experts, and in the early eighteenth century it seemed proper to make a serious effort to discover everything that was scientifically possible about Siberia: coasts, rivers, mountains, minerals, soils, plants, animals, people. In 1733 a systematic exploration which included seven separate expeditions commenced, and for many years the reports were coming in, to be studied and classified and published. It was in the course of these expeditions that Chelyuskin explored the most northerly coasts of Asia, and Behring the straits that separate Asia from America, and thus put their names on the map. So by the middle of the

eighteenth century, the government in St Petersburg had a very good idea of the size and resources of their property east of the Urals.

Using those resources was quite a different matter, mainly because of the difficulties of transport. Furs remained about the only commodity that was light and valuable enough to make the transport worth while. There were rich mineral deposits in the Altai region, for example, but attempts at mining and smelting could not develop into anything big.

Another problem was shortage of inhabitants. It would need an enormous migration to fill that space, and the people simply were not available. Russian peasants were mostly bound to stay with their landlords, who needed them on their farms in Russia. The Tsar formed some peasants into Cossack groups to settle in difficult frontier areas, but this was more to hold the land than to develop agriculture and industry. The very size and remoteness of Siberia could be used, though, as a safe way of storing prisoners. People who had opposed the Tsar's government but who had not been condemned to death were often sent to live in distant parts of Siberia, and sometimes prisoners of war found themselves enlisted willy nilly in the Russian army and sent to a distant garrison. When the nineteenth century began, the Tsar held Siberia firmly, but it did not seem that its value and importance bore much comparison to its size.

The Russian Empire in Asia

In the nineteenth century the Russians pushed forward their frontiers in Asia as far as they could. This was partly because they were now strong enough to do so, and the steady improvement of weapons increased their advantages over Asiatic foes; partly because they feared the ambitions of other European powers (just as the others feared Russian ambitions, so that it became a matter of grabbing territory to prevent a rival getting her hands on it); partly it was the old story of one event leading to another. The Russian advance can be divided into three main theatres: the Caucasus, Central Asia and the Far East.

For many centuries Cossacks and Russians had waged war against Tartars and Turks. The feud went back to the years when Jenghis Khan's hordes had ravaged Russia and reduced the Russian principalities to vassal states. By now the tide was strongly in the other direction. The Tsar's armies had reached the Black Sea and hammered the Turks every time there was a war – which was quite often. The so-called Eastern Question that arose from the decline of the Ottoman Turkish Empire and the pressure of Russia in the Balkans is a complicated part of European international history which is not part of our story here; but it caused a number of wars, the best-known being the Crimean when Britain and France helped Turkey. Caucasia lay between the Russian and Turkish empires. It was a land of towering mountains and of forests, but also of fertile valleys and plains. From ancient times conquerors had passed that way, Greeks and Persians, Romans and Byzantines, Mongols and Turks, and there were also many different small nations and tribes who had made their homes beside the mountain ranges. The result was a baffling patchwork of languages, customs and religions. The Caucasian peoples seemed to have only one thing in common; they were all brave, warlike and independent.

When Russian troops attacked Turkish forces in that area they usually won big successes and seized much territory. The Russian advance was welcomed by two Christian nations who lived south of the mountains and who had long suffered from attacks by Turkey and Persia, their large Muslim neighbours. To Georgians and Armenians the Tsar appeared as the great protector of Christians. In other parts of Caucasia the Russians met desperate resistance from Muslim peoples. Here the Tsar's army found itself at war not against badly led and badly trained Turkish soldiers, but against fierce and fanatical warriors who were brilliant horsemen and fighters, led by chiefs who proved themselves masters of guerrilla tactics. Only after a costly struggle lasting thirty years were the Russians able, in 1858, to force the Imam Shamyl, their greatest enemy, to surrender. After this the whole Caucasus region, up to the frontiers of Turkey and Persia, became an obedient part of the Russian Empire.

Across the Caspian Sea from Caucasia the steppes of Central Asia spread eastwards towards the mountains that marked the frontiers of Afghanistan and the outlying provinces of the Chinese Empire. This was the heart of the Eurasian land mass, the centre of the Old World. It contained famous old cities that had long been strongholds of Muslim culture and art, most notably Samarkand and Bukhara. Strategically it was an important area, and the Russian government did not trust the people who lived there. The nomad peoples of the steppes were unsettled and unruly, and the khans and emirs of the cities were fickle and cruel (which was partly because they themselves felt threatened). Many Russian officials thought that there was no alternative to taking over this whole troublesome area. An additional reason that pressed them on was that another European power

A meeting of Circassian leaders on the banks of the Ubim River in the Caucasus. From E. Spencer, 'Travels in Circassia', 1839.

Russian expansion in the Caucasus and central Asia during the nineteenth century

Shamyl and his two surviving sons, photographed in 1859 at St Petersburg. They are wearing Caucasian costume, which was soon copied by many Cossacks. Shamyl had been fierce and ruthless, but never treacherous or sadistic, and the Russians treated him with respect and admiration.

seemed to be interested in the same area; Britain from her empire in India. (The British authorities in India, on their side of the mountain barrier, feared that the Russians were hatching plots to stir up the Afghans.)

The conquest of Central Asia took place mainly during the 1860s and 1870s. It was not easy, for some of the peoples who lived there were warriors who knew how to make good use of the Russians' transport difficulties, especially in the deserts. But modern weapons won. The last people to resist were the Tekke Turkomans, who routed a Russian army outside their fortress of Gök Tepe in 1879. In 1881 the Russians took Gök Tepe; they lost 300 troops in the attack, and killed 20,000 Turkomans. It had been a war of merciless killing on both sides, and the victorious General Skobeloff explained: 'I hold it as a principle that in Asia the duration of peace is in direct proportion to the slaughter you inflict upon the enemy. The harder you hit them, the longer they will be quiet afterwards.' Whether or not this was true, peace came to the region, and within a few years modern cities were being built beside the old, and the European residents could go by tram to the opera house along the boulevards of Tashkent.

The third area of expansion was beside the Amur and into the Manchurian fringes of the Chinese Empire, as we saw in Chapter 3. The man who drove forward here was Nikolai Muravyeff, a young nobleman whose political ideas were liberal by Russian standards but who had a large imperial vision of the importance of Siberia and of the need to give it a good outlet on the Pacific. In the words of his nephew Mikhail Bakunin, later famous as an anarchist, the Pacific was 'the Mediterranean of the future'. Muravyeff met the Tsar and so impressed him that he appointed him governor of Eastern Siberia in 1848. He pushed settlers and troops down the Amur, but he did not have to fight. As we saw on page 42, he was able to seize the time when China was too weak to resist, and get by negotiation all that he wanted. Vladivostok – the name means 'ruler of the east' in Russian – gave the desired outlet. Before the century was over, Russia dominated Manchuria and gained another harbour, in milder waters, at Port Arthur.

The Russian government, however, was realistic. To hold Siberia and the whole of northern Asia was one thing, to try to expand into a different continent was another. Russia had claimed Alaska and permitted traders to settle there in the late eighteenth century, but now decided that she could not hope to hold so distant and sparsely populated a colony, which was not very valuable anyway. In 1867 Russia sold Alaska to the U.S.A. for 7,200,000 dollars.

Vassili Vassilievitch Verestchagin, 1842–1904, tried to make his pictures as realistic as possible, and studied war at first hand – he was decorated for his part in the fighting at Samarkand, and died when the battleship 'Petropavlosk' was sunk by a Japanese torpedo. Here are two of his Samarkand paintings of 1869–72. One shows local warriors guarding the entrance to Tamerlane's mausoleum, the other a Russian sentry looking down on the main street of the city.

The Russian Empire in Asia was being rounded off, but it was still very short of people and its huge resources were scarcely being tapped. After the freeing of the serfs in Russia in 1861, a growing number of peasants thought that it would be better to try their luck in the east than to stay in old Russia, where they still found life hampered by rules and regulations and debts. In the 1880s the government decided that it would be wise to help would-be colonists to settle in Siberia, and the annual number of immigrants rose steeply: 25,000 in 1887, 92,000 in 1892, and the stream went on. Now at last it seemed that agriculture and industry could begin to grow.

One thing was still making it difficult to 'develop' the gigantic land. Transport still relied mostly on rivers and on roads that were little better than tracks. Obviously railways were needed, and some of the Tsar's advisers had been urging this since the 1850s, but nothing was done. This was partly because it could cost so much, partly because the government did not want to upset other powers, like Britain, who would suspect that the Russians' real intention was to use railways for military purposes. At last, though, the need was so great that such arguments had to be swept aside. The Tsar found a man who seemed to be strong enough to face the huge task, and the Trans-Siberian Railway was begun in 1891.

The man was Serge Witte, son of a German-born official and a Russian general's daughter. He was intelligent, ambitious, brutally efficient and unpopular. He was the man to drive ruthlessly over difficulties and opposition. Instead of inviting companies to build the railway, as had been done, for example, in the U.S.A., he decided that the state should do the job itself, raising the money and employing the workers. His enemies objected that it was not part of the state's duties to engage in business, to become a capitalist. But Witte took no notice. He was appointed Finance Minister in 1892 and succeeded in raising large loans, especially in France which had just signed an alliance with Russia. Witte was in a hurry. He drove his men on, through difficult country and often appalling weather. He did not bother with a double track – a single track, with loops here and there for trains to pass, would do at

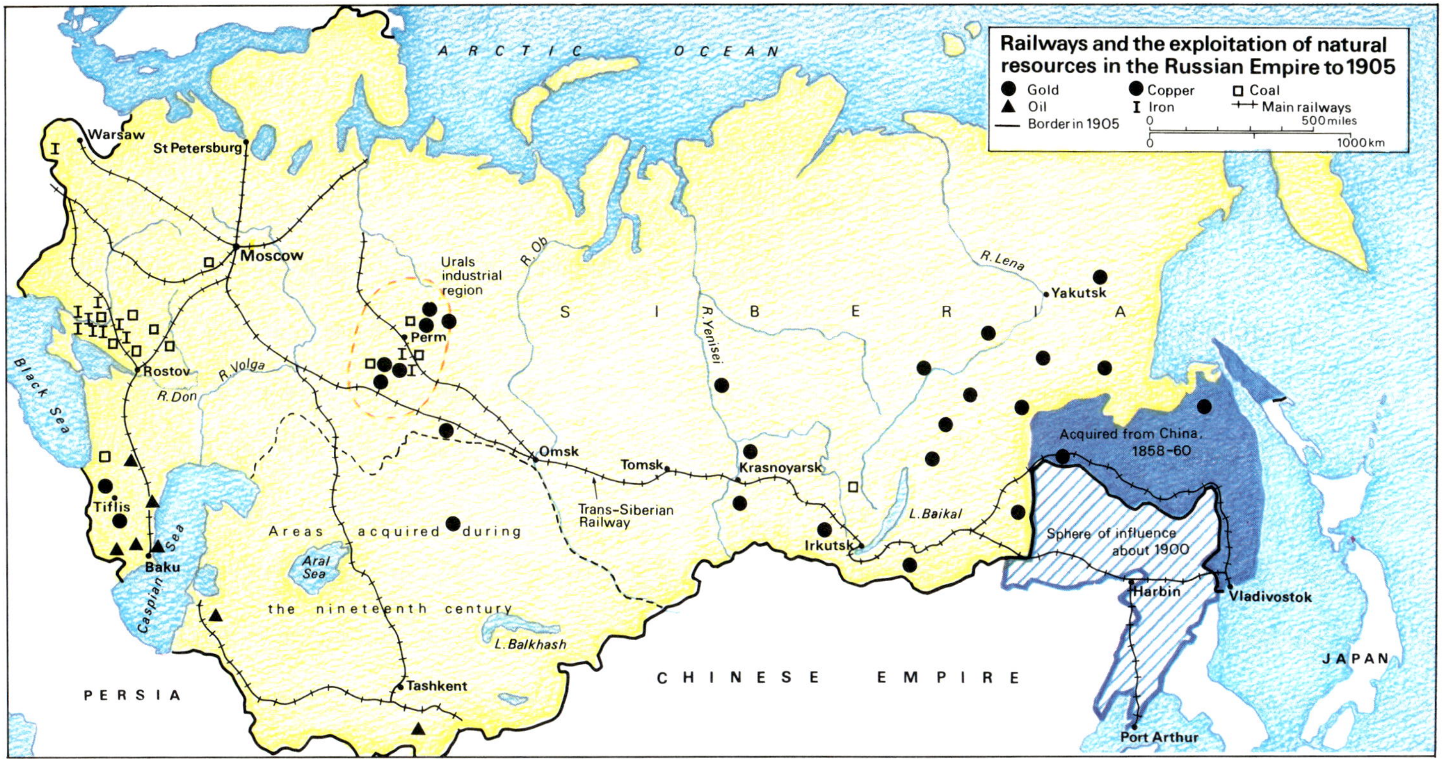

An artist's impression of a typical scene at a halt on the Trans-Siberian Railway.

first. He knew that the whole railway would need reinforcing and improving soon, but calculated that it was so necessary that it would quickly make a huge profit, and this would pay for the improvements. The important thing was to get it into action quickly.

The Trans-Siberian Railway was ready for use in only thirteen years. It was just in time to carry troops to the battlefields of the Russo–Japanese War, and its single track was barely adequate; it had never been intended for this sort of strain. But, in spite of its unhappy opening, it was a vital step towards developing Russian Asia. Russia was a very different society from the U.S.A., Siberia was vaster than the American West, the railway came later and there were, as yet, not many enterprising businessmen rushing to make fortunes by developing the forests and minerals. The young U.S.A. had grown so rapidly that it almost seemed as if Russia, the old giant, was not making any progress at all. In fact, the huge empire was now consolidated and had at last reached the point when it could begin to exploit its huge resources.

6 Partitioning Africa

In the later part of the nineteenth century there were not many parts of the world left for European powers to take. Only the land mass of Africa and the islands scattered over the vastness of the Pacific were largely free of white rule or influence, and the Pacific islands were no problem, for they could easily be gathered under the 'protection' of any naval power that decided it needed a few.

In Europe the powers had varied policies on overseas possessions. The old colonial powers of the sixteenth century, Portugal and Spain, were perforce content to hold and consolidate, if they could, what was left of their empires. Their old rivals, the Dutch, spread and strengthened their rule in the East Indies until, by the end of the nineteenth century, they held most of the huge rich Indonesian archipelago – Java and Sumatra, Celebes, the Moluccas and even part of New Guinea. The U.S.A. and Russia were mainly engaged in spreading into the wide lands that lay beside them. Britain held the sea-routes of the world and was planting an astonishing number of new white states all round the globe; could she possibly want more? Some European states, like Austria–Hungary and Sweden, did not think that colonies would be of any use to them. There remained three contenders for colonies in the lands that were still available: the old imperial power of France, and, after about 1870, the two new great powers, Germany and Italy.

France overseas

Even after being defeated by Britain in North America and India, France of the old regime retained a valuable empire, including many islands which supplied tropical crops. Napoleon had little interest in colonial empires, though he was a great builder of empire nearer home; before becoming master of most of Europe he had tried to build an empire in the Near East, and might have succeeded if the British navy had

above: *Zouaves of the 1830s, from a contemporary French illustration.*

below: *The French landing at Sfax, Tunisia, 1881, from a contemporary newspaper illustration. By now automatic weapons were giving even greater advantages to European forces; this is a Hotchkiss gun mounted in the bows of a naval steam launch.*

not cut his communications and isolated his army in Egypt. French governments in the nineteenth century, when they thought it necessary to improve their prestige by gaining military glory, naturally looked across the Mediterranean.

In 1830 France picked a quarrel with the Dey of Algiers and invaded his land. Whatever France's motives, no European state was likely to complain. For three centuries Algiers had been a pirate city, the base for corsairs who seized Christian shipping, raided Christian coasts and took Christians as slaves. Complaints to the Dey and naval blockades and bombardments only brought temporary improvements, and France was doing a service to all Europe by ending this pest.

Taking Algiers proved quite easy. But behind the coast lay the mountains of Barbary, home of the fierce and independent Berber tribes. They had never been very respectful to the Dey of Algiers and they were certainly not going to obey the Christians. There was a ferocious guerrilla struggle until 1847, when Abd-el-Kader, the greatest leader of the Muslims in Algeria, surrendered. But savage risings flared up from time to time for many years afterwards. South of the mountains began the Sahara desert. Nobody could tell how much of this could be reckoned as part of Algeria. For the rest of the century French columns pushed slowly from oasis to oasis, building forts and trying to make the nomads live peacefully under French orders. It proved a difficult task.

The long-drawn-out fighting that eventually brought most of north-west Africa under the French flag was only partly done by French troops. Algerian regiments were raised, the *Turcos*, and soon they were joined by Europeans who wore Algerian uniform, the *Zouaves*; they were supposed to be very dashing and were imitated in one or two other lands – most strangely, perhaps, in the U.S.A. during the Civil War. But undoubtedly the troops who became most identified with the fighting in North Africa were the Foreign Legion. The Legion was not raised specially for Algeria, and fought in many lands; indeed, its proudest episode, the defence of the hacienda of Camerone, which it still celebrates each year, took place in Mexico when Napoleon III was trying to set up a puppet empire there in the 1860s. But the work in North Africa, with its boredom, hardship and cruelty, seemed to the French authorities especially suited to their foreign soldiers, and this is where the Legion became a legend.

French influence soon became strong further east. In the

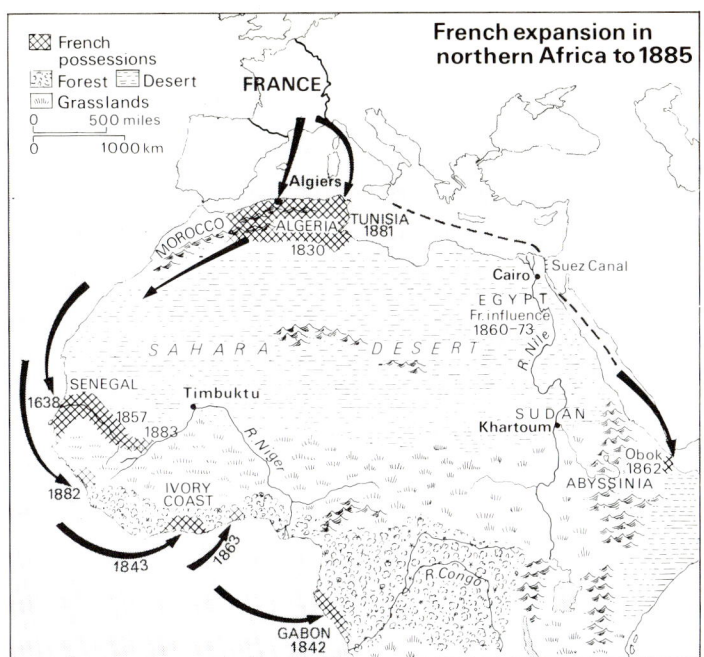

1850s Napoleon III's attempts to intervene in the affairs of the Turkish Empire resulted in the Crimean War against Russia. The Middle East was what diplomats call a sensitive area, because it was on the way to India and the Far East. It became even more important in the 1860s when a French engineer, Ferdinand de Lesseps, achieved something that had been considered as long ago as the days of the pharaohs. He dug a canal big enough for ocean-going ships between the Mediterranean and the Red Sea. The Suez Canal ran through Egyptian territory, and the Khedive of Egypt (who was nominally a vassal of Turkey but acted as an independent ruler) held a great many of the shares in the company that owned and operated it. French influence, of course, was also strong, and it was Napoleon III's wife who performed the opening ceremony.

The canal made an enormous difference to shipping between Europe and the East. Sailing ships still found it better to use the long route around the Cape, but for steamers which did not depend on winds and whose owners profited best by quick passages, the new shorter route was now the only one worth using. This was obviously extremely important to

The opening of the Suez Canal, 1869, from 'The Illustrated London News'.

Britain, and in 1875 the British prime minister, Disraeli, bought the Khedive's shares on behalf of the British government. His purchase gave Britain a controlling interest in the canal, and thus obliged her to interfere in Egypt to put down an anti-European rising in 1882; so that it was Britain, not France, that became the leading European power in the north-east part of Africa. Many French politicians resented what Britain had done, but because France's military might had been crushed by Germany in 1870-1 their resentment had to be bottled up.

Possessing an overseas empire was seen by some Europeans as indicating a country's importance and this was partly why France went ahead in north-west Africa. She also seized a large part of Indo-China, in spite of Chinese and local resistance, and took possession of some Pacific islands. There were relatively few French people willing to settle in any of this empire except Algeria, only a short distance across the Mediterranean from Marseilles. France wanted overseas possessions partly for trade and partly to give her influence in the affairs of the world. For the same reasons Germany and Italy now began to look for overseas empires.

The dark continent

In the middle of the century, at the time when the triumphs of European invention and industry were being displayed in the Crystal Palace in Hyde Park, the cliché about Africa was still largely true. Behind the coastline most of the continent was still unknown to Europeans. This was mainly because it did not seem to them that there was much wealth to be gained from Africa. The people seemed too poor and ignorant to buy much. The only valuable product was slaves, and that trade was now outlawed. It was difficult to get into Africa, too. There were some big rivers, but they were not easy to sail up. There were no real roads, and the rough tracks were often narrow lanes through jungle, where everything had to be carried by human beings. Apart from the Boers (page 28) the only Europeans who went to Africa stayed close to the coast.

Two sets of people came in different fashions to shed light. There were missionaries, anxious to bring what they believed to be spiritual light to the natives of Africa, and there were explorers who set out to discover scientifically the answers to geographical questions and so illuminate for European eyes the mysterious fastnesses of the continent. Sometimes the

Posed studio portraits of two of the most famous explorers of Africa which manage to convey a good deal of the personalities and interests of the two men. David Livingstone, 1813–73, Scottish medical missionary and geographer, is seen with globe, book and paper, and his cap and walking stick. Henry Morton Stanley, 1841–1904, Welsh-American journalist, is in full explorer's costume, complete with gun and African servant-boy.

same man filled both roles. The reports they sent back to the Churches or the learned societies that had supported them, newspaper articles and the books they wrote not only informed the geographers, but fascinated millions who read books and papers and attended lantern lectures.

On the map the wavering criss-crossing of the explorers' routes may give the impression of aimless wanderings. In fact, almost every expedition had a definite goal; perhaps to reach the 'forbidden' city of Timbuktu where the Sahara caravans gathered, or to discover the source of the Nile somewhere in the centre of Africa, and the reasons for its floods. This in itself made exciting reading, but the tales told by the explorers were even more thrilling. Everything was vast and wild, rivers and mountains, jungles and plains and deserts. There were amazing and dangerous beasts, and often the natives were just as amazing and dangerous. There were pygmies and cannibals, people with saucer lips and elongated necks. There were kings who butchered their subjects for the most trivial offences, or merely to test new weapons, and there were witch-doctors whose mysterious mumbo-jumbo reduced their tribes to abject terror.

This was the picture that ordinary Europeans formed of Africa and the Africans. They usually did not understand much. Probably they knew the difference between the so-called 'Arabs' of the north and the 'Negroes' who filled the rest of the continent, but there was little knowledge of the very wide differences between the many races within each of those two rough classes, and very little insight into the reasons and meanings that lay behind apparently strange customs. The study of anthropology had not spread far in Europe. What Europeans did see clearly was that the Africans were a very long way behind in science and technology, that they could not read and write and that they knew little about the rest of the world. Their religions seemed to be primitive superstition, their art and music crude and barbaric. It was tempting for white men to see only these things and to feel very superior, and many of them did.

Once more it was possible for European colonisers to boast that they were doing a great service to the people they came to rule. They were going to bestow on the natives a knowledge of modern European civilisation. Whether they were right or wrong, honest or hypocritical has been argued ever since.

Meanwhile the centre of Africa was already being penetrated by others. Early in the century ambitious rulers of Egypt had sent soldiers up the Nile and had claimed the boundless expanse of the eastern Sudan as part of their realm. It was poor and sparsely populated, but it did not cost much to rule; soldiers and officials were paid little or nothing, and expected to make up for this by taking as much as they could from the local people. Government consisted of collecting bribes and enforcing obedience by merciless floggings and executions. Slavery was supposed to be stopped, but the slave trade was the most lucrative business in the Sudan, and the officials were hand in glove with the slave-dealers. In the later part of the century Egypt stretched her outposts further still, into Equatoria, and at the same time the Khedive began to employ Europeans to govern parts of the Sudan and to try to stop corruption and slaving, but this was a near-impossible task.

Other slave-dealers were plunging deep into Africa from Arab settlements along the east coast, Zanzibar being the biggest slave market of all. The slave-raiders, most of them not real Arabs, but blacks employed by the Arabs, swept away all the people and property in district after district; the people who were not caught or killed fled, the cattle were eaten or driven off, the crops and buildings burnt. With the slavers

A Hottentot woman with her baby, working for a Boer family, drawn in 1812.

Gang of captives met at Mbame's on their way to Tette: this is Livingstone's caption for the illustration from his book 'The Zambesi and its Tributaries', published in 1865.

The only African people who succeeded in defeating a white attempt to conquer them were the Abyssinians. This picture of Menelik and his chiefs appeared in 'The Illustrated London News' four weeks after the battle of Adowa, where they had defeated the Italians.

pushing further to get at places they had not already wasted, there seemed to be nothing to prevent them from ravaging the entire population of central Africa, except for those tribes who were too warlike to be enslaved – and these often found it profitable to help the slave-raiders.

Perhaps there was indeed a need for civilised powers to step in. But there must have been some Europeans, as they read accounts of travel in darkest Africa, who noticed how rarely peaceful white travellers were harmed by the 'savages', and how often they received loyalty and kindness – even from the slave-raiders. There may also have been some who wondered how much of the troubles could be traced back to trade with Europe. It was white merchants who kept on asking for ivory, for palm-oil from West Africa and spices from the plantations of Zanzibar, and offering in exchange goods that included strong drink and guns.

The scramble for Africa

The two maps on page 85 show the speed with which some of the European powers grabbed at pieces of Africa, and why the process has been called a scramble. Once it became clear that several powers were taking an interest, each began to feel that she would have to hurry to prevent the others from grabbing the best bits. At first some governments were unwilling. For example, Bismarck, the German Chancellor, did not see that his country had any need for colonies. But there were others in Germany who wanted 'a place in the sun', and eventually they got their wish. One method by which would-be imperialists influenced their governments in Europe was by persuasion; by pressure in newspapers and in political meetings, by beating the drum and waving the flag and suggesting that their country could not be great unless it had colonies. Another method was to set up trading companies which would get permission from African rulers to trade in their territories. Sooner or later there would be disputes with local people, because frontiers were very vague, and with companies from other European countries, and this would force the government to intervene.

France naturally expanded from her earlier footholds in north and west Africa until she was able to link most of her possessions in one great block. Germany, starting from scratch, had to go for areas that had not already been pre-empted. She managed to find varied places which could probably supply different sorts of tropical produce, though much of German South-West Africa was desert. By the time Italy came into the contest she had little choice, and made for the 'horn' of Africa where she established rule in Somaliland and Eritrea and persuaded Abyssinia (Ethiopia) to become her protectorate. In 1896, however, there was a disaster. An Italian army advancing into Abyssinia to suppress a revolt was routed with

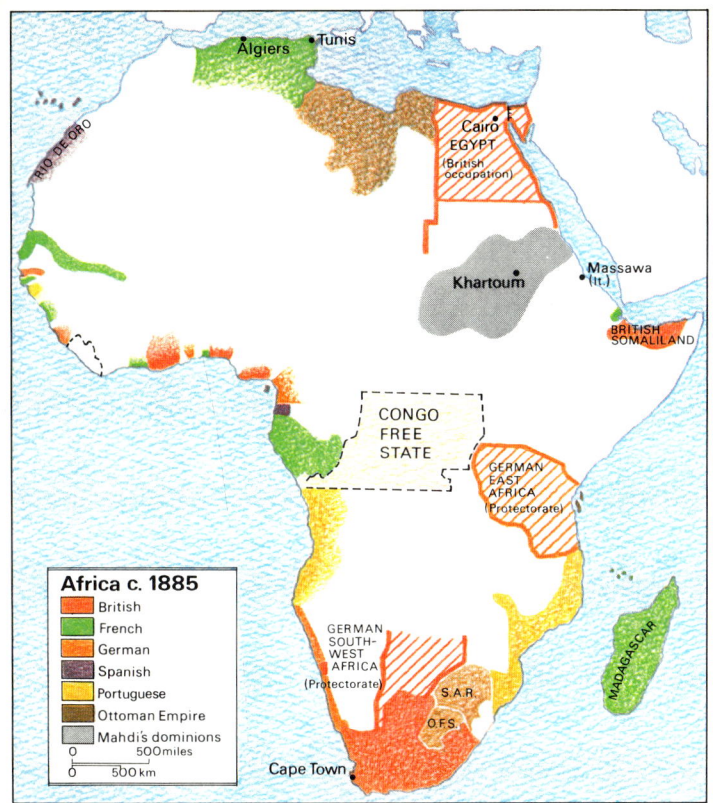
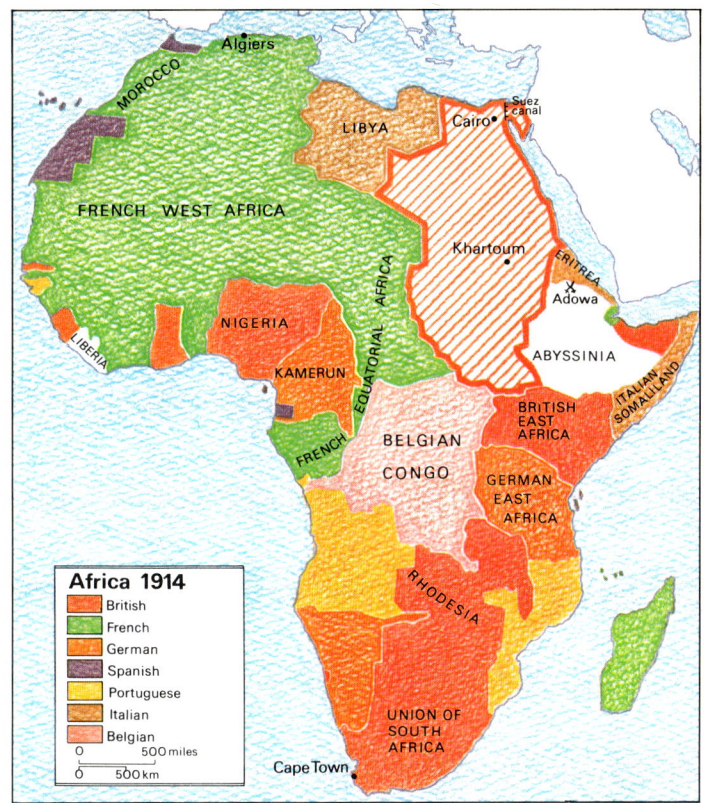

very heavy losses, and Abyssinia became once more a fully independent kingdom. Italy partly compensated herself by seizing Libya from the Turkish Empire in 1912. By 1914 Abyssinia and Liberia (a small republic that had been set up as a home for liberated slaves in 1820) were the only parts of Africa not under white rule or 'protection'.

There was one large area that was taken over, not by a European government, but by a private company; though the head of that company happened to be King Leopold II of Belgium. He set up the Congo Free State in 1885 with the consent of other European governments. Leopold's company was interested only in making money. It destroyed the Arab slave trade, but only to enslave the population itself. Natives were forbidden to collect rubber or ivory except for the state. Then, in 1892, they were ordered to work for the state as a substitute for paying taxes. This forced labour soon became oppression of the worst sort. People who failed to produce what was expected of them were severely punished, and there were revolts that added to the cruelty and suffering. Gradually rumours of what was going on began to trickle out of the remote areas where the worst atrocities were being inflicted, then foreign consuls made reports and at last Leopold had to order an official investigation; its report confirmed how very badly the Congo Free State had been run. In 1908 the Belgian parliament voted that the Congo should henceforward belong to the Belgian state, and conditions began to improve.

In several of the colonising countries there were people who seemed to become more ambitious as their colonies grew. Looking at the map, they felt that they ought to strive towards certain 'natural' objectives. Some French felt that they had a right to extend all over the Sahara and Sudan to the Red Sea, and resume their influence in Egypt. Some Germans and

Not all Europeans took the idea that they had an imperial duty to spread European civilisation in wild places very seriously. These cartoons of the jungle before and after being improved by German discipline appeared in 1896 in the Munich paper 'Jugend'. It seems that the cartoonist thought it absurd for Germany to get deeply involved in Africa, but perhaps he was also a Bavarian seizing an opportunity to scoff at Prussian habits.

Portuguese felt that it would be good if their colonies on the east and west coasts could be extended to meet in the centre, and give them broad belts running right across the continent. In one country, Britain, there were some with an even more grandiose ambition, one which cut across the schemes of the others. This was to drive ahead in Africa until Britain held a broad belt of territory stretching from south to north; in a phrase popular at the time, 'from Cape to Cairo'.

The man who was most dedicated to this dream of British empire in Africa was not a politician, but a very successful business man named Cecil Rhodes. He had migrated from England to the diamond fields of South Africa, and had done so well that his company, De Beers, came to dominate the entire diamond trade of the world. Rhodes thought in world terms. He believed that it would be best if the world were to be led by the Teutonic, especially the Anglo-Saxon, peoples, and hoped for co-operation between the British Empire, the U.S.A. and Germany. Meanwhile Britain should advance to fulfil her imperial destiny in Africa.

Rhodes was able to convince some influential British politicians and officials that he was right, and he also had the wealth to be able to move ahead of the government. In order to strike northwards he founded the British South Africa Company to trade and mine in the lands of the Mashona and Matabele peoples. By 1895 the Company ruled all that land, and named it Rhodesia. Rhodes was also now Prime Minister of the Cape Colony.

There was one great obstacle to Rhodes' plans: the Boer republics. They were as independent-minded as ever, and suspected Rhodes. In 1886 a rich goldfield was discovered in the Transvaal, and there was a gold rush. People of all nations came, many of them British. A new town called Johannesburg soon had 100,000 inhabitants. Some of them became very rich. The Boers did not like these newcomers, these *uitlanders*, or foreigners. They made them pay taxes but would not allow them to become citizens with full rights, for fear that they would prove so numerous and powerful that they would destroy the old Boer way of life. Ill-feeling grew on both sides, and Rhodes plotted to use it. He arranged that there should be a rising of the uitlanders against Boer 'oppression', and that his friend Dr Jameson, with 600 armed men, should ride to Johannesburg and take charge. The 'Jameson Raid' of 29 December–2 January, 1895–6, was a complete fiasco. The uitlanders did not rise, Jameson and his force were all captured by the Boers. The result was that Rhodes had to resign, disgraced, from the leadership of the Cape Colony. The Boers were more suspicious than ever, but also confident that they could beat the British. There grew up a feeling that sooner or later there must be a war to decide whether or not Britain ruled all South Africa.

At about this time Britain was advancing rapidly from the other end of Africa. Her troops were moving up the Nile, into the Sudan and towards Equatoria. This was the end of a story that had started in 1882, when a Sudanese holy man had proclaimed himself the *Mahdi* (the guided one), the final great prophet of Islam, and raised a holy war against the Egyptians. His followers, fanatically brave, with their simple weapons routed and massacred half-hearted and demoralised Egyptian troops. In Egypt, though there was still an Egyptian government, Britain had only just taken control as a supervising power and was not eager to get involved in a new war. So the Sudan was left to the Mahdi. Unfortunately the British officer sent to organise the withdrawal of the last Egyptians, General Charles Gordon, disobeyed his orders and tried to hold the capital, Khartoum. The Mahdi took Khartoum on 26 January 1885, and Gordon was killed. A British relief force arrived

The last moments of General Gordon, Khartoum, 26 January 1885. This life-size tableau was put on display at Madame Tussaud's Waxworks, London, in 1898, the year Gordon was avenged, and remained on show until 1941. (In fact the Mahdi had ordered that Gordon should not be harmed.)

The 'Fuzzy-Wuzzies' were the Beja tribes who lived near the Red Sea coast of the Sudan, nicknamed because of the way they dressed their hair and famed for their fury in battle. Osman Digna was their leader for the Mahdi, a man of the Hadendowa tribe who had been a merchant, had travelled and proved a cunning general. On 13 March 1884, a British force from Suakin advanced towards the Beja camp at Tamai. The British marched in two squares. Suddenly 'Fuzzy-Wuzzies' leapt from a concealed gully and attacked. One square broke and retreated, leaving behind its machine

just too late, and retreated. People in Britain blamed the Prime Minister, Gladstone, for having delayed; thought Gordon a Christian hero and martyr; believed the Mahdi to be a barbarous tyrant; and wanted revenge. But it was many years before a combined Egyptian and British army set about the reconquest of the eastern Sudan.

It took the British about ten years to realise that there could never be peace until the Sudan was conquered. The Mahdi's successor, the *Khalifa* (the successor) saw his duty as constant war against all unbelievers, Muslim, Christian or any others, so there was no option but to fight. Besides, the British were aware of French and Belgian expeditions towards the upper part of the Nile, and they wanted to get there first. An Egyptian and British army under Sir Herbert Kitchener began to advance up the Nile in 1896, and the decisive battle was fought outside the Khalifa's capital of Omdurman, just across the river from ruined Khartoum, on 2 September 1898. During the long reign of Queen Victoria, British soldiers fought some very brave enemies all over the world, and the Mahdists were probably the bravest. They also greatly outnumbered the British and Egyptians. But they sacrificed themselves in vain against magazine rifles, machine-guns and quick-firing artillery. A couple of weeks after the battle the British commander, Sir Herbert Kitchener, pushed on south and found that a small French expedition had arrived from the west at Fashoda. He politely but firmly pointed out that this was Egyptian territory, and the French must leave. Henceforward the whole course of the Nile, from the Mediterranean to the middle of Africa, was to be under British control.

At the southern end of the continent the decisive war that so many had been expecting between Britain and the Boers broke out in October 1899. Most European states sympathised with the Boers, who looked like a small nation fighting to preserve its freedom against a greedy empire.

guns. But the other square held firm, the broken square rallied and retook the guns, and at last the Beja fled, leaving about 2,000 of their men dead. The British lost about 110 dead and the same number wounded. The paintings, by Douglas Giles in 1885, try to show what the battle looked like from both sides.

Besides, some European powers had been rivals of Britain for bits of Africa, and would be quite pleased to see her checked. Was it possible for the Boer David to beat the British Goliath? The Boers knew the country, and were accustomed to spending long hours in the saddle and to using their rifles as ordinary everyday tools. They were well armed; taxes from the goldfield had paid for excellent Mauser rifles and Krupp cannon, and the Boers' sympathisers in Europe did everything possible to supply them. There seemed to be a good chance that the Boers might overwhelm the British forces in South Africa before reinforcements could arrive.

The Boers lost their chance, partly by halting in order to besiege unimportant British garrisons like Ladysmith and Mafeking. Then the British in their turn tried to advance, and they were at first beaten back with heavy losses in a series of battles; the Boers, lying in cover among their rocky hills, acquired a great reputation for marksmanship in picking off their assailants. Soon, though, the weight of the British Empire told. Reinforcements came sailing to South Africa from British dominions and colonies as well as Britain itself. To the exultation of people in Britain, the Empire rallied to help 'the Mother Land'. The besieged garrisons were relieved – there was hysterical rejoicing in Britain at the relief of Mafeking especially – the British armies captured the Boer towns and the Boer army surrendered. By September 1900 Britain had won.

Yet the war went on. Small independent forces of Boers, known as *commandos*, began a highly successful guerrilla war. Very swift, helped with supplies and information at every Boer farmhouse, they seemed able to strike when and where they wished and almost always escape. At last the British decided that the only way to defeat the commandos was to cut them off from their supplies. The British divided up the land with barbed wire fences and blockhouses, and cleared out all

For the British soldiers the later part of the Boer War was mainly a dull grind of sitting in small blockhouses or chasing commandos, with a good chance of being raided or ambushed. This photograph shows soldiers building a blockhouse.

For civilians forced to leave their homes there were refugee camps for those thought harmless and concentration camps for those who might help the commandos. This picture from 'Navy and Army Illustrated', May 1901, shows rations being issued to refugees at Bloemfontein.

the Boers from their farms. These people, mostly women and children, were brought together, or concentrated, in camps. The concentration camps were badly run, and of the 120,000 people forced into them, about one in six died of disease or hardship. It was a policy that earned Britain the deep hatred of many Boers, and severe criticism in Europe. In the British Parliament the government was accused of employing 'methods of barbarism' to bring the Boers to their knees. Right or wrong, however, these methods succeeded. On 31 May 1902 the Boer representatives signed the Treaty of Vereeniging, and their land became part of the British Empire.

It was the British intention to win over the Boers, to bring them to accept their new position willingly instead of merely on paper. There were grants to help to rebuild the farms destroyed in the war, and South Africa was given its own government very quickly. The Union of South Africa, where there was equality between the English and Dutch languages and the people who spoke them, came into being as a self-governing member of the British Empire exactly eight years after the Peace of Vereeniging. If all went well, here was another new white nation growing up within the British family.

It had taken about thirty years for the whole continent of Africa and all its peoples, excepting only Abyssinia and Liberia, to be shared out among European states, with the lion's share going to Britain.

7 The white man's world

In 1897 Queen Victoria's empire was the greatest the world had ever seen, her navy the most powerful, her capital city the most populous and rich. It was here in London that her Diamond Jubilee was celebrated with all the pomp and splendour that Britain could provide. It was a celebration not only of the queen's 'sixty glorious years', but also of British power, of 'dominion over palm and pine'.

Among the thousands who watched the processions go by and tried to identify the different troops who paraded in endless variety, from every colony and dominion, there were probably few adults who did not reflect on the changes that the past sixty years had seen. It was a common theme in the commemorative editions of newspapers and magazines that were being sold as souvenirs of the Jubilee. Coaches and horses had given way to steam railway trains, and now there were a few petrol engines spluttering along the roads in horseless carriages. The sailing ship was disappearing, the seas belonged to the iron steamer and the armoured battleship. Messages sped with the speed of light across country on telegraph wires and under the sea by cables, and cheap postal services linked families who had members scattered in new lands all over the world.

Contingents of soldiers from every part of Victoria's world-wide empire took part in the Diamond Jubilee processions and parades. Here the Queensland mounted rifles form the escort for a royal carriage, forming a contrast to the British cavalry in their ceremonial uniforms who line the road.

To commemorate the Diamond Jubilee 'The Illustrated London News' issued what it called 'a record number of a record reign', which began by declaring the past sixty years to have been both 'a Triumphal March' and 'a time of transformation'. This is one of the pictures from that issue.

In 1890 Stanley published an account of his latest expedition entitled 'In Darkest Africa', and it was a best-seller. It provided a manufacturer of the new electric lights with an idea for an advertisement, humorously but confidently assuming that everybody admired the white man's ideas of progress. But there were a few who did not; some artists felt that Western civilisation was worn out, and that life was more true and beautiful among peoples whom the whites called primitive. The best-known of these was the French painter Paul Gauguin, 1848–1903, who went to Tahiti in 1891 and spent most of the rest of his life in the Pacific islands. This is one of his paintings called 'Te Rerioa' (Daydreaming).

Four years later, when the new century began, there was every sign that this progress was going to go further and faster. In 1901 Marconi succeeded in sending wireless messages across the Atlantic, and two years later the Wright brothers made the first aeroplane flight. These were only some of the most obvious signs of progress. There were steady improvements in food production and in every sort of manufacture and in medicine. People were living better and longer, and governments were more and more taking the responsibility of looking after those members of the population who were not able to take care of themselves.

All this was the work of the European nations, either those who dwelt in Europe itself or those who had arisen from colonies planted in other continents.

The great strength that the white men derived from their inventions and industries made them masters of the world, as the maps on page 96 show. In technology, and especially the technology of war, they were superior to all others. But did this entitle white people to feel that they were altogether better than other races? Many of them certainly did think this. They believed that their material power was the result of mental power; they had invented and improved the machines, they best understood how to use them. Some would carry the argument further. They would say that all this was because European civilisation was better than any other; the mixture that had somehow matured from the ideas of the Greeks and Romans, the medieval Church, the Renaissance and the Enlightenment was better than anything other civilisations could offer. Some assumed without much thought that because the white man was strong he must be right, while others thought that they could prove it reasonably.

So the Europeans who ruled or dominated most of the other peoples in the world did not hesitate to impose their ways. Even the civilised peoples of Asia had much to learn about the white man's ideas on law and government, trade and industry. As for the more primitive peoples, they had to be instructed in the elementary qualities of civilisation. Some regarded this as a sacred duty:

A war correspondent reporting from the Sudan in 1887 saw a Pear's soap sign on the rock that marked the furthest point of the British advance. The cartoonist of 'The Illustrated London News' interpreted the story like this.

> 'Take up the White Man's burden –
>   Send forth the best ye breed –
> Go, bind your sons to exile
>   To serve your captives' need;
> To wait in heavy harness
>   On fluttered folk and wild –
> Your new-caught, sullen peoples,
>   Half-devil and half-child.'

So wrote the English poet Rudyard Kipling, who had spent his youth as a journalist in India, and there were many men and women who agreed, both British and other Europeans.